WHY DID GOD MAKE ME?

Why Did God Make Me?

Finding Your Life's Purpose
Discernment in an Evolutionary World

LOUIS M. SAVARY AND PATRICIA H. BERNE

Paulist Press
New York / Mahwah, NJ

Cover image by kenjito/Shutterstock.com
Cover and book design by Lynn Else

Library of Congress Cataloging-in-Publication Data

Savary, Louis M.
     Why did God make me? : finding your life's purpose : discernment in an evolutionary world / Louis M. Savary and Patricia H. Berne.
        pages cm
     ISBN 978-0-8091-4871-4 (alk. paper) — ISBN 978-1-58768-360-2
     1. Theological anthropology—Christianity 2. Self-actualization (Psychology)—Religious aspects—Christianity. 3. Spiritual exercises. 4. Savary, Louis M. New spiritual exercises. 5. Teilhard de Chardin, Pierre. 6. Spiritual life—Catholic Church. 7. Ignatius, of Loyola, Saint, 1491–1556. Exercitia spiritualia. I. Title.
     BT701.3.S29 2014
     233—dc23

                                                                            2013047649

ISBN 978-0-8091-4871-4 (paperback)
ISBN 978-1-58768-360-2 (e-book)

Published by Paulist Press
997 Macarthur Boulevard
Mahwah, New Jersey 07430

www.paulistpress.com

Printed and bound in the
United States of America

This book is dedicated to the memory of
Father Pierre Teilhard de Chardin, SJ
(1881–1955)
His unique life purpose was to offer to contemporary
people a spiritual path that integrated their faith traditions
with the discoveries of modern science and the theory
of evolution. His insights provide the inspiration
and grounding for the concepts and
structure of this book.

Principle and Foundation

You were created to make a unique contribution to the great evolutionary project initiated and continually supported by God, namely, bringing all creation together into one magnificent conscious loving union.

Since all other things in the universe share with you this common eternal destiny, they are essential to and inseparable from you as you participate in the pursuit of that ongoing evolutionary process.

Individually and joined with others, you are to use all means available to promote and carry out this shared purpose with all your personal creativity, compassion, and energy, always seeking and choosing what is more conducive to that purpose.

For this, God empowers you to grow in passionate love and care for all elements of the cosmos, since they, as you, all live and move and have their being in God's love.

The New Spiritual Exercises: In the Spirit of
Pierre Teilhard de Chardin

CONTENTS

CONTENTS

Many years ago, a friend of ours, a multimillionaire at thirty-five, happened to pick up a book on philosophy. As he was paging through it, he noticed a question that he felt was being proposed to him: *What is the purpose of human life, and your life in particular?*

It was a wake-up moment. "Why am I here on Earth?" he asked himself for the very first time. "What am I meant to be doing with my life?"

He wondered whether others had been confronted by those powerful questions.

That afternoon on the golf course with two of his millionaire friends, he asked them, "What do you see as your purpose in life? What do you want to accomplish?"

Without much hesitation, one who owned seventy-five fast food franchises said he hoped to acquire seventy-five more of them. The other who owned about fifty large apartment buildings said he hoped to acquire fifty more.

Our friend realized that his two companions saw no other purpose in their lives than to accumulate more possessions and to become richer and richer. Realizing that, until that moment, he had been quite like them, he decided that day that he wanted his life to have more meaning and purpose than merely increasing his wealth. Yet he also realized that he had not found that new purpose for his life.

He eventually found it, but it took him nearly twenty years before he could clearly identify it.

The process of recognizing and identifying your unique purpose in life is called *discernment*. Suppose you are faced with a major choice between two good opportunities—such as two good job offers—and you wish to know which option would be more in line with your destiny, that is, what you were meant to do with your life. Identifying the opportunity you were meant to choose requires discernment, because each choice will lead you on a different path.

Logic, reason, or even your family and your friends may advise you to take the more advantageous option or to make the safer choice. But your destiny—or life purpose—may be calling you to choose the other option. Only a discernment process will help to clarify which way to go.

Our friend's two golfing companions chose to continue on the paths they had been following. They had never questioned or challenged the idea that their life's purpose might be anything other than amassing possessions and making money. In contrast, our friend realized that there must be something *more* than that purpose for his existence on Earth.

What he lacked back then was a simple and orderly way of discerning and identifying his unique life purpose.

In this book we offer such a way. It is a step-by-step process that anyone may use to clarify his or her unique life purpose. And it won't take twenty years. It won't even take a week.

The life purpose discernment process is described in part 2 of this book. Part 1 explains the theory behind the process. It tells how and why the process makes sense. But if you are eager to start the process, go directly to part 2. You can always read part 1 later on.

Louis M. Savary
Patricia H. Berne
Tampa, Florida
Easter Sunday 2013

ACKNOWLEDGMENTS

In this book we as authors mention a number of people who have helped us shape and carry out our life purpose. We encourage you to create your own list of acknowledgments, including all those, past and present, who have helped you in your endeavors to pursue your unique life purpose.

We offer special thanks to Peter and Barbara Peloso, who introduced us to Herbert Alphonso, SJ's, discernment book, *Discovering Your Personal Vocation*, which expanded the discernment process of the original Spiritual Exercises and inspired us to do the same in our book *The New Spiritual Exercises: In the Spirit of Pierre Teilhard de Chardin*. And thanks to all the people who throughout these past seventy or more years struggled to keep the ideas of Teilhard alive in the church and the world.

Some colleagues who read the manuscript and gave us comments include Roger Yaworski, SJ, Roger Haight, SJ, Richard Hauser, SJ, and Matt, Sheila, and Dennis Linn.

Thanks to Paulist Press, our publisher, especially our editor Donna Crilly, who "went to bat" for our manuscript and found a way to make it happen.

We love our many family members who allowed us to use their stories. Others whose stories we used, openly or in disguised form, include Clare Crawford-Mason, Robert Mason, Jefferson Vander Wolk, Sandy Cahill, Dr. Marta Schneider, Andre Auger, Sheryle Baker, Peter and Mary Esseff, Robert Fritz, Steven Halpern, Muriel James, and Margaret Miller.

We honor the many deceased family, friends, and others who guided our lives and purposes in both small and significant ways and whose memories and stories surface for us now and then. We like to call them God's "angels" because they gave us a push at the right time and in the right direction.

We thank Frank Frost, Sister Julia Marie Hutchison, SND, Sister Janet Doyle, OP, Rev. Robert O'Donnell and the staff at Saint Joan of Arc Church, Orleans, Massachusetts, among others, who support and promote our work in many ways.

Extra-special promoters include Rev. Len Piotrowski and the staff at Saint Paul Church, Tampa, Florida, for their enthusiastic support of all we do.

We honor all those who recognized their unique calling (as well as those who never recognized it for what it really was), yet had the courage to pursue that uniquely personal and divinely inspired purpose, even though others tried to discourage, stop, or hinder them in its pursuit. We thank them for having been the instruments of divine Love and for remaining true to their unique purpose in life.

INTRODUCTION

Perspective

For centuries in Christian tradition, it was assumed that every individual on Earth shared essentially the same life purpose, namely, "to save one's soul." In this traditional language, one had to love God, keep the Ten Commandments, and do good works, because that was the way to achieve one's purpose in life, which was to attain "eternal salvation." To most people, "salvation" meant to be admitted, when you died, into a heavenly kingdom where God lives, a place that exists somewhere beyond the stars.

But the discoveries of modern science challenge us to redefine, enlarge, and expand on that traditional life purpose. It seems clear that there can and should be much more meaning and significance to each human's life on Earth.

According to scientific research, and especially the theory of evolution, this Earth of ours and the rest of creation seem to have been around for billions of years before the human race appeared. According to the most recent scientific calculations, the universe was born almost fourteen billion years ago at the moment scientists call the "Big Bang." And evidence suggests that our Earth came into existence only a little more than four billion years ago. More surprisingly, in Earth's long evolutionary history the appearance of human beings turns out to have been very, very recent.

Most of us can't imagine fourteen billion years—or even four billion. But a simple comparison may be made by using a more familiar measure of time.

Suppose the fourteen-billion-year life of the universe were to be summarized in one Earth year, 365 days. Using that measure, the Big Bang would have happened during the first moments after midnight on January 1, and our home planet Earth would have come into being only around the middle of September. The very first forms of life on our planet would be seen in October. However, human life as we know it would not have appeared on Earth until the last day of the last month of that year, that is, on December 31, during the last few seconds before midnight. Each second of our symbolic year represents, roughly, a hundred thousand years.

Someone once observed, "We are custodians of but a tiny fragment of Earth's story."

So, what was going on in the universe during all those eons of evolutionary time before *Homo sapiens* appeared?

It seems rational to assume that in the beginning the divine Creator Spirit had a purpose for creation. As we now begin to see, that purpose has been developing and evolving during those eons of time. We might say that we have begun to realize that the divine Spirit that permeated creation in the beginning has set in motion within the universe an evolutionary plan or "project." In other words, divine creation, the universe, was on the move; it was incomplete, and it was developing. This plan or process of development had already been well under way for billions of years before we humans arrived on the scene. As someone put it, "We are finite actors in an infinite narrative."

Some of the clearest expressions of evolutionary development through millions of years on Earth were countless life forms—plants and animals—growing continually more complex and conscious. Most recently, we humans emerged on Earth.

Pierre Teilhard de Chardin, a devout Jesuit priest-scientist (1881–1955), was one of the first to recognize this long-term divine project and what it might mean for spirituality and for Christian theology.

Teilhard couldn't deny the "ancient-ness" of the universe

and Earth and the relatively recent appearance of humankind on the planet. Nor could he deny the evolutionary processes scientists were observing going on at every level of being and life. And this evolution clearly seemed to have a direction and a purpose. After all, Teilhard argued, our universe started from a Big Bang made up of countless, lifeless subatomic particles and photons of light, and has evolved to a planet Earth where there are today almost seven billion living, interacting human individuals capable of self-reflective consciousness. Quite an evolutionary process! From particles to people. From simplicity to complexity. From inanimate matter to millions of life forms. From unconsciousness in metals and minerals to sensory awareness in plants and animals to self-reflective consciousness in humans.

If all these scientific discoveries are true, Teilhard reasoned, then the information they offer must be able to be integrated into theology. And that's what Teilhard did. He put all of it together—the findings of modern science, the theory of evolution, and Christian theology.

After years of reflecting, and being inspired by Saint Paul's writings, Teilhard realized that creation is moving with direction and purpose, and he characterized that direction as forward and upward toward higher and higher levels of ability and consciousness. The human race never seems to cease exploring, to try to break old records, to increase life expectancy, to find cures for deadly diseases, to go farther faster, to conquer outer space, to take the next step into the unknown.

Teilhard saw that not only humans but every particle of the universe is part of a divine plan, or project, for creation. He realized that plan has been in process since the beginning of time, and that we humans are an essential part of that plan.

Essentially, that divine project involves shaping the cosmos—and humanity with it—to become, what Saint Paul called a "new creation."[1] Paul also described this project as "building the Body of Christ."[2] In Paul's vision, all of us individuals are incorporated into one universal divine body as its members.

During the twentieth century, Teilhard took Paul's idea of "building the Body of Christ" and expanded it to cosmic size.

Teilhard began to realize that (1) *this evolutionary project was really the most important ongoing event in the cosmos*, and that (2) *humans had a large and essential purpose in furthering this divine project.*

So, the assumption here in seeking to identify your life purpose is that *your life purpose will always involve helping promote this grand evolutionary project that began on the first day of creation, and you will do it by helping to bring that project one small step further toward its fulfillment.*

Saint Paul described the fulfillment of the divine cosmic project as the universal Body of Christ coming into its fullest maturity.

In John's Gospel, Jesus describes this fulfillment when he prays, saying, "Father, my prayer is that all of these [who follow my way] may become one as you and I are one, that they themselves may become one [in me and in us]."[3]

LOVE: THE DRIVING FORCE

For Jesus, the nature of divinity is Love, all-embracing Love, an infinite life force that is not only compassionate and forgiving but also endlessly creative. That divine Love, as Teilhard says, is the driving force behind creation and the driving force moving the entire evolutionary process forward and upward toward that perfect loving union of all beings. At every moment, Love, that divine creative energy within all things, is urging onward all the evolutionary processes going on throughout the universe toward its true fulfillment.

One of Teilhard's greatest gifts to us was recognizing this underlying generative power of Love guiding the universe's evolution. He knew this driving force of Love had to reflect the action of the divine source of all being, who, according to John the Evangelist, is pure Love and pure Intelligence.[4] This divinely intelligent Love would find expression even in fragmented, inanimate things, like elementary particles and such nonliving chemical elements as gases, metals, and minerals.

Teilhard had to wonder: What would "love" mean to electrons, protons, and neutrons? And he had to grasp—and try to formulate—a divine law that could keep all creation, inanimate and animate, moving in a continual evolutionary trajectory toward higher levels of complexity and consciousness.

What Teilhard discovered for us was a first formulation of the divine Evolutionary Law that has been guiding creation since the moment of the Big Bang, the start of space/time, nearly fourteen billion years ago. In its fullest expression, this Evolutionary Law—or driving force built into creation—might be stated as the Law of Attraction-Connection-Complexity-Consciousness.[5]

THE EVOLUTIONARY LAW

This law that Teilhard formulated is an evolutionary expression of the divine law of Love. They are two ways of expressing the same law, because the Evolutionary Law, when followed, will ultimately bring all creation, through evolution, into one conscious loving union. It is a law—supported by divine Love permeating all creation that keeps everything and everyone uniquely who they are. Yet, in the end, we will all become one loving Cosmic Body, bringing to fulfillment what God envisioned for us—and for creation—from the beginning.

This Law of Attraction-Connection-Complexity-Consciousness is at the heart of creation's project. This law is what drives creation forward and upward. This is the law that will help complete the grand cosmic project.

Therefore, if we wish to align our lives with what the divine Spirit is doing in the world, we will want to promote and build our lives around this Evolutionary Law of Love: Attraction-Connection-Complexity-Consciousness.

We can use this law at three levels. Not only can (1) our everyday spirituality and spiritual practices be guided and governed by this law, but (2) so also can our major decisions in life. And in this book, we go even one step further: (3) *We use this Evolutionary Law to help you discern your unique primary life purpose.*

The discernment process described in part 2 of this book suggests a step-by-step way that the Law of Attraction-Connection-Complexity-Consciousness may be used to discover and confirm your unique life purpose.

The divine Spirit of wisdom that permeates all things is helping you to identify your purpose as you move through each stage of this process. You are being urged on by that Spirit and nourished by the divine Presence. The drive to make a positive difference is written into your heart and programmed into your genes. You are being continually invited to keep making your special contribution to the grand project. You are being supported and guided all along. Carrying out the self-revelatory process in part 2 is, in part, your response to that call.

The self-discovery process involves reflection on each of these four evolutionary stages—*attraction, connection, complexity,* and *consciousness*—as they affect your life. It is a process that takes much thought and prayer, so it is recommended that you carry it out with a pen and a notebook to record your responses to many proposed questions.

This book offers two approaches to finding your personal life purpose. First, the book can be used independently as a guide in a personal exploration to search for, identify, or confirm your life's purpose. It may also be used during a formal retreat based on the book *The New Spiritual Exercises: In the Spirit of Pierre Teilhard de Chardin*, in which the primary objective of the retreat is discerning your life purpose.[6]

NOTES

1. See 2 Cor 5:17 or Eph 2:15.

2. See 1 Cor 12:12, 27; Col 2:19b; Eph 4:13.

3. John 17:21. See also John 17:15–26.

4. According to John, the three divine persons in the Christian Trinity are *Father/Creator* (Love; see 1 John 4:7–21), *Son* (Logos, or Intelligence; see John 1:1–5), and *Holy Spirit* (Life-Giver and Wisdom-Giver; see John 14:15–28).

5. Teilhard simply called it the law of *complexity-consciousness*. But much of his writing on evolution also discusses the forces of *attraction and connection*; therefore, I believe it would make the Evolutionary Law much more self-evident, clear, and complete to add these two earlier stages to the law's formulation.

6. Louis M. Savary, *The New Spiritual Exercises: In the Spirit of Pierre Teilhard de Chardin*. New York: Paulist Press, 2010.

PART I

A
DIVINE
PERSPECTIVE

CHAPTER 1

YOUR LIFE HAS A PURPOSE

Daredevil Nik Wallenda has become the first person to walk across Niagara Falls on a high wire.

Tens of thousands of people gathered at the falls and millions more were believed [to be] watching on television as Wallenda crossed some 200 feet in the air on a two-inch-wide wire strung over the raging waters of Horseshoe Falls, the largest of the three falls that make up Niagara Falls.

Wallenda trotted in his final steps across the wire and stepped into Canada, barely 25 minutes after he started.

After he greeted his wife and family, Wallenda was approached by customs agents, who asked him for his passport, which he presented.

"No, I'm not carrying anything over. I promise," he said.

"What is the purpose of your trip, sir?" the agent asked.

"To inspire people around the world," Wallenda said.[1]

Nik Wallenda's unexpected response to the Canadian customs agents shows that his amazing feat was far more than an ego trip for him. It was a symbolic accomplishment for all of us. It was an expression of physical, mental, emotional, and spiritual discipline and determination, to show that people, if they want to, are capable of achieving greatness. He wanted his daring deed to motivate people to make a positive difference, to stretch themselves, to develop their talents and abilities.

That high-wire walk was an expression of his life's purpose: to inspire people to go beyond the ordinary, to aspire to do what has not been done before. His feat was a call to the greatness in all of us.

The same is true for all of the athletes at the Olympic Games. Their accomplishments are a challenge to us to find our inner greatness and not to settle for less than our highest potential for good.

You and I may not be called upon to walk a tightrope over Niagara Falls or to qualify for a spot on the Olympics team, but each of us throughout our lives has contributions to make—small and large—that will foster the growth and development of the human community. Each of us has a unique personal life purpose, a destiny for which we were born, a destiny that has to do with contributing to the increase of love in the world. Do you know what things you can contribute uniquely to this reservoir of love? Have you committed to making your contributions?

At some point, most self-reflective persons have asked themselves questions like *Why was I born? Why am I here? What is the meaning of life and my life in particular? Do I have a purpose? Is there anything special about me? Do I have a contribution to make? Does my life have any importance? Can I really make a difference?*

At the same time, others go through life never asking such questions. They simply live from day to day. Nevertheless, even the unreflective have specific purposes in life, though they may never try to identify them. They may carry them out in different ways without ever knowing it. For example, they may smile or be kind to someone one day, and their smile or kind word may be enough to reverse someone's plan to commit suicide; and that person who had been considering ending life may turn out

4

later on to make a significant contribution, or perhaps many contributions, to the world.

Some years ago a fifteen-year-old girl, who grew up in an abusive home, was arrested for shoplifting and put into a juvenile detention home where she worked in a cold basement laundry. Most adults there simply assumed she would be just one more person who would be in trouble with the law all her life. However, one attendant looked past the girl's anger and defiance, noticed her love of music, and brought her a guitar—a gesture of recognition and love. Partly because of that gesture, the young girl grew to become the world-famous Irish singer and songwriter Sinéad O'Connor. Today, she has enlarged her life purpose beyond show business to become a worldwide advocate for women's rights.

Most reflective people cannot live without looking for personal answers to the questions. "What is *my* life purpose?" and "Is my life part of a larger purpose?" They ask themselves these questions because, without a purpose to provide motivation and personal direction, they would lack a focus for their energy and potential. It would be like a ship lacking a rudder and without a destination. To them, it becomes crucial to find answers to those fundamental questions.

Some try to uncover their purpose by studying philosophy. Others hope to find it in pursuing a career, climbing the ladder of success. Others simply desire to contribute something to the world and hope that what they are doing has some significance. Many parents find purpose in raising their children and providing for them the benefits they themselves might not have had. Others find meaning in scientific research and the pursuit of knowledge. Others find deep meaning in patriotism and in serving their country as defenders of freedom. Many find meaning in helping others through teaching or tutoring, nursing, counseling, or volunteering in needed services or causes. Still others turn to the creative arts—literature, painting, design, music, and even entertainment—to fulfill their purpose.

Perhaps most people turn to religion to find meaning and purpose and to discover how they are part of a larger plan. They believe that the Creator Spirit in whom we live and move and have our being has a purpose for each of them and that this permeating divine Spirit has a larger purpose in mind for the human race and for creation. These people believe they have been put on Earth for a reason. They want to do what they believe is being asked of them. As the Lord's Prayer puts it, these people would say to God:

Thy kingdom come.
Thy will be done on Earth....

Such people believe that the sentence "Thy will be done on Earth" means there is work for them that needs to be accomplished on Earth, that they are meant to make a positive contribution to life here and now. They believe that their earthly purpose is not simply to qualify for a blissful life after death but also to make a difference during their days on Earth. They realize that doing their part in transforming the world is the only way God's reign will ever come to fulfillment on our planet, the only way *Thy will be done on Earth* will be accomplished.

You Can Discover Your Life Purpose

We write this book for those who wish to find their life purpose—and their place in a larger plan—and have not yet been able to identify it clearly. We write also for those who would like to reassure themselves that they are fulfilling their life's purpose, that they are doing what they were destined to be doing.

From a divine perspective, every human being, believer or not, has a personal and unique purpose in life. The challenge for each one is to discover that purpose. For all of us, it will usually involve making a positive difference in the world, and, we hope, leave the world a better place than when we arrived.

Some people discover their primary purpose in life at a very young age, as Patricia's daughter did at age seven. Suzanne knew even then that she wanted to be a writer, a creator of stories. And that's what she does today. Others find their true purpose only later in life, as did our friend Jeff, who spent most of his adult life as a businessman, but only later discovered he was meant to share his life's wisdom as a philosopher.

Some seem to have one major purpose, like Dr. W. Edwards Deming who, all his life, taught people "how to work smarter, not harder." Single-mindedly, he was still leading workshops for business leaders on this theme in his nineties.

Many others, like our friend Clare, seem to have many different purposes and projects, though upon reflection these seemingly different purposes often reveal a common theme running through all of them.

Some inventors, like Guglielmo Marconi, Alexander Graham Bell, Thomas Edison, Steve Jobs, and other communication innovators, have life purposes that involve making major contributions to the development of society. Most others' life purposes—like those of parents, teachers, family doctors, and health care workers—are fulfilled quietly and, for the most part, go unnoticed except by the relatively few of us whose lives are touched by them.

Some will have a purpose that they accomplish by themselves, like many famous writers who struggle alone to formulate their ideas and stories. Most of us will have a purpose that involves others, one that we could not accomplish by ourselves. Even the symphony composer, who works in solitude to put his musical ideas on paper, needs the many musicians of an orchestra and a conductor to give life to the musical markings on the page.

Some people, like Albert Einstein, will become famous during their lifetimes because of what they contribute, while others, like Pierre Teilhard de Chardin, who died in 1955 and whose insights gave rise to this book, will make contributions that are not recognized until long after their deaths.

The contributions of everyone, recognized or not, are important in the grand divine plan.

NOTE

1. Alice Gomstyn and Michael S. James, "Niagara Falls High-Wire Walk: Nik Wallenda Crosses Falls, Fulfills Lifelong Dream." *ABC News*, June 15, 2012.

CHAPTER 2

YOUR PURPOSE IN AN EVOLUTIONARY WORLD

Your Purpose in a Static World

Today, we understand in a new way the meaning of "Thy will be done on Earth" primarily because, thanks to modern science, the vast majority of human beings have moved in their thinking from a static worldview to an evolutionary view. Most of the world's religions and their beliefs, however, were formulated many centuries before science transformed the traditional understanding of creation. And some religions have not yet caught up with what we now know about how the universe actually came to be the way it is.

We can assume that early scriptural writers and other thinkers, operating without the knowledge of modern science, had to guess at how the world got started. It is one thing to believe that a divine Creator created the world, but to describe what actually happened in those earliest moments at the dawning of creation had to be imagined—made up—because many centuries ago, no one had the slightest idea of the origins or vastness of the universe as we are coming to know it.

From ancient times, just about every religion and culture produced its own version of a creation story—how the world came to be. In those stories, although many different versions were recorded or handed down, the stories had certain elements that were similar. For example, in all of them, the Earth was the center of the cosmos; it was a world where, once all the elements of creation were in place, not much really changed. Things on Earth this year would be very much the way they were last year, and next year things would again be very much the same as before. That is, to them creation was cyclic, yet unchanging.

A static and cyclic world is one in which nothing truly changes significantly, and everything goes through the same cycles again and again. Sunset follows sunrise each day. Seasons follow seasons each year. Parents have children; those children grow up to become parents and have their own children, and so on.

According to this viewpoint, in the beginning God created the Earth and the creatures on it exactly as they appear today. In this traditional story of creation, nothing has really altered its appearance. Right from day one, cows looked exactly the way they do today. So did dogs, cats, horses, owls, lobsters, frogs, and fish. From the beginning, men and women looked much as they look today. From the beginning, the mountains, the rivers, the seas, the deserts, and all the rest of nature looked much as they do now. The seven continents were exactly where they are today. The oceans were exactly the same size and shape as they are now. The Grand Canyon was created as a canyon. The Rocky Mountains were created as mountains. This view of the world is summarized in the well-known saying, "There is nothing new under the sun."

In our times, science has led us beyond a traditional worldview where nothing changes very much except to move in cycles into an *evolutionary* worldview where everything is always in process, mostly going forward and upward. Only recently are religious traditions catching up to this transformation.

In past centuries, especially for believers, their lives' purposes were already defined for them by their faith traditions. They might have formulated it, as many Christians did in these or similar words:

> *Every person was created*
> *to praise, reverence, and serve God,*
> *and by this means to save one's soul.*

This identical definition of everyone's life purpose—to *save one's soul*—may have proved sufficient in a fixed and cyclic world, where it was assumed that Earth was the only planet that existed and was therefore the center of the universe. Given this definition of life's purpose, Earth probably was seen as little more than a testing ground for God-fearing humans hoping to graduate from a temporary life on Earth to eternal life with God in Heaven.

There is nothing wrong with having the purpose of desiring to live forever in divine Love's embrace, but perhaps it is rather an incomplete purpose, given what we are beginning to learn about our Earth from science. What we are discovering about the evolving universe makes the divine creative Spirit so much more awesome and reveals a much richer purpose to our years on Earth. We are invited here and now to participate in helping realize an immense divine plan *as well as* the opportunity of enjoying eternal life with and within Love Itself.

We are given the privilege of helping make that grand divine plan a reality. As long as we are breathing, God has work for us to do in furthering that plan.

Your Purpose in an Evolutionary World

The traditional static and cyclic worldview has been over-turned during the past few centuries, especially during the past 150 years. Thanks to science, we now know that our Earth is not the center of the universe. We are a minor planet orbiting a minor star, the Sun, in the Milky Way galaxy, a galaxy that may contain as many as a hundred billion more Suns like ours. In the known universe there are billions of galaxies, each with billions of stars like our Sun.

As all creation is developing in a continuing evolutionary process, so is our Earth. Every level of being on our planet is in evolution, even at a very fundamental inorganic level.

If a space traveler looked down upon Earth many millions of years ago, as we now can thanks to modern science, that traveler would have seen a single great continent, named *Pangea* by contemporary scientists. This massive continent slowly broke apart to form the many continents of our planet as we know them today. We also know that these continents rest and ride on a series of tectonic plates that are always shifting in slow motion beneath the Earth's crust. When these tectonic plates collide, as they often have over many millions of years, their collisions form various mountain ranges and gave birth to volcanoes. Because of continuous tectonic motion over many millennia, some mountains are much older than are others. Our planet Earth has also gone through a series of ice ages, the last of which ended about nine or ten thousand years ago. We know, too, that our four-billion-year-old planet was essentially lifeless for much of its first billion years of existence. During its second billion years, single-celled organisms—bacteria, viruses, molds, and fungi—became Earth's earliest citizens and its only living inhabitants. Mutated versions of these original evolving organisms remain with us to this very day.

All life on Earth began in the sea and, after millions of evolutionary years, strange, now long-extinct creatures evolved and emerged from slimy waters to climb upon the land. Millions of years later, dinosaurs emerged, ruled the planet for almost sixty million years, and then went extinct—all of this many millions of years before the first humans appeared.

The many species of dogs we see at the pet store or dog shows today evolved from one species of wild wolf. At their evolutionary start, horses were as small as dogs.

In our own lifetime, we watch all forms of civilization continuing to evolve—cultures, technology, manufacturing, transportation, communication, language, law, medicine, music, art, literature, entertainment, education, government, and information storage.

Even the human organism that is called *Homo sapiens* is a product of evolution. Archeologists who study the hominid lines of evolution tell us that close to a dozen attempts to form humanity as we know it were tried, failed, and went extinct. The most recent extinct hominid species were the Neanderthals, who managed to endure, according to some estimates, through three hundred thousand years. Today, *Homo sapiens* is the only hominid race on the planet, though some of us still carry about 2 percent of Neanderthal genetic material in our human DNA. Behaviorally, modern humans emerged about fifty thousand years ago. But it was less than twenty thousand years ago when our ancestors first gave birth to cities, civilization, complex languages, and culture.

In our own day, the evolutionary process seems to be speeding up. For example, it took the human race thousands of years to reach a life expectancy of forty-four years at the beginning of the twentieth century, yet by the beginning of the twenty-first century, within a span of only one hundred years, life expectancy has doubled to eighty-eight. In the world of communication, amazing evolutionary strides have been made. In the past 150 years, we have developed from the handwritten letter to the telegraph, the telephone, the phonograph, the tape recorder, the fax machine, the computer, the Internet, the smart phone, and so on. Instant, even face-to-face communication anywhere in the world or in space is available.

All this information leads to the realization that the created universe is evolving, not static. As this new evolutionary information is being assembled and assimilated, we begin to realize that the divine Spirit that gives existence and life to all things must have some investment in the evolutionary process Earth and its creatures are going through. Otherwise, why would a supremely loving and intelligent Creative Force spend almost fourteen billion years to get creation ready for humanity to emerge on planet Earth? *There must be some direction for creation, some project or plan, some purpose or direction for all that divine effort and guidance over all those eons of time.*

As we reflect on the long process of creation, it becomes clear that Earth cannot be merely a testing ground or classroom preparing us for heaven. It must be much more. Creation itself, especially our planet, seems more likely to be a divine experiment or a divine project with a purpose and a direction.

Thus, for humans, our individual lives on Earth must somehow be involved in this divine project. This leads us to realize that our life purposes cannot be merely to save our individual souls. Rather, together with all of humanity, our purpose is more likely to involve helping further this divine evolutionary project on Earth and to help complete it. So, taking this divine project perspective into consideration, we might formulate the human person's life purpose in a new way:

> *You were created to make a unique contribution*
> *to the great evolutionary project*
> *initiated and continually guided by God.*

With this new formulation of human purpose, there is no need to stop praising, reverencing, and serving God, as we did in the older formulation. It's simply that we are called upon to learn to praise, reverence, and serve the ever-present divine Spirit from a new perspective. We have come to realize that we can better serve the Creator's purpose by helping to accomplish the divine work on Earth.

What happens on Earth, to the planet itself and to the people and life forms on it, is important to an all-loving Creator and should be important to us. The divine Spirit driving the universe is also working through us. In responding to this grand project, we are responding to an inner personal call to make our unique contributions.

What happens to our Earth and to the human race is so important that in searching for our life purpose, we come to realize that when we find our life purpose, we discover that it is all tied up in helping fulfill the divine purpose—or will—for Earth and humanity. *Thy will be done on Earth.*

CHAPTER 3

EACH ONE'S LIFE PURPOSE IS UNIQUE

Each one's life purpose is unique, yet everyone's life purpose is meant to promote the divine evolutionary plan for creation, that is, to accomplish the union of all sentient beings through love.

It seems clear from the nature of this divine project that not all individuals would have the same personal life purpose—no more than every employee in a grand hotel would have the same set of functions to perform—but that each person would have something unique to contribute to such a vast and all-encompassing plan.

In the running of a hotel, there are managers, marketing people, bookkeepers, cashiers, valet parking drivers, luggage handlers, receptionists, phone operators, concierges, mechanics, laundry staff, supply clerks, housekeepers, cooks, wait staff, dishwashers, and a host of others who help make the hotel run smoothly. And while the hotel's overall purpose is to care for its guests, those guests are looking to the hotel staff to understand and provide for their many reasons for being there—food, rest, entertainment, clothing care, meetings, ongoing travel, guidance around town, and other services.

In a similar way, the Creator's divine project has a wide variety of important purposes to accomplish in order to fulfill its destiny. It needs explorers, inventors, writers, artists, scientists, mathematicians, philosophers, physicians, counselors, coaches, psychologists, clergy, communicators, educators, entertainers, parents, and many others who strive to push us toward the next evolutionary stages of human living.

Every loving parent is involved in this push to improve conditions of life for their children and grandchildren. If parents fail to foster the healthy development of their children, and perhaps even use or abuse them, we hope that a loving educator, counselor, or a member of a faith group will find ways to begin to heal the physical and emotional wounds the child may have sustained at home.

Pat tells a sad story that happened during her childhood. It seems two of the neighborhood boys, about eleven or twelve years old, were playing alone in one boy's home. The boy discovered his father's gun, and the two of them were fascinated with it. Not knowing the weapon was loaded, the friend playfully pointed the gun at the boy and pulled the trigger, killing his friend.

Perhaps in a static world, people might call the incident a tragedy and label the boys as "bad." Perhaps, others might condemn the boys for playing with a weapon and blame the father for leaving a loaded gun around the house. The father would be expected to live with guilt all his life. Both pairs of parents would be inconsolable at the loss. The child who pulled the trigger would be traumatized and permanently scarred emotionally.

In an evolutionary perspective, we try to see a larger picture. What kind of consciousness could the incident evoke in the neighbors? What did the two families and the neighborhood learn? How did the community grow through this tragedy in compassion and awareness?

What happened in the neighborhood, Pat recalls, was evolutionary. First, there was an outpouring of compassion. Neighbors came with words of consolation, along with gifts of food for both families. Instead of condemnation, awareness was raised. People showed forgiveness and understanding to the child who had pulled the trigger. Neighborhood children became conscious that it was not wise to play with guns, that guns are not toys. Neighborhood parents began to lock their weapons away from their children while becoming more aware of how and where their children were playing. Members of the community were reshaping their neighborhood in positive ways, not merely lamenting what had gone wrong and looking for people to blame.

Among humans, the reward and punishment mentality reflects a very primitive level of consciousness and morality. Similarly, this vast divine project cannot have as its destiny simply the separation of "good" people from "bad" people. Such a limiting effort implies that the divine Spirit who created the universe is primarily a petty, judgmental divinity focused only on reward and punishment. Rather, a deity whose divine nature is unconditional love and all-embracing forgiveness can have no lesser divine purpose than a project that would bring all creation together into one magnificent conscious-loving union.

Your contribution to this divine project will be something only you can do, because only you are here in this specific time and place to do it. Yet, in the larger evolutionary picture, your unique contributions, no matter how small they may seem, will further the grand divine purpose, to move humanity onward and upward in love.

It follows that if you love the divine Spirit that gave you life and purpose and want the great love project to succeed, you would want to find out how you can best help further the progress of this divine purpose. You would ask yourself:

> *What role(s) does God want me to play in helping to fulfill the divine evolving project for creation? What purpose can I best carry out to help bring all creation together into one magnificent conscious-loving union?*

It may be important to note that your purpose may or may not be directly related to, or dependent upon, your state in life,

19

that is, whether you are married, single, clergy, or in consecrated religious life.

If we truly lived in a static and cyclic universe, people would merely have to discern a life vocation—married, single, clergy, or vowed religious—and carry it out according to the rules governing that state in life. Yet, even in a static world, some people experience more than one of those vocational states at various times in their lives. For example, a religious sister or brother may leave religious life and get married. A married person may lose a spouse through death or divorce and become a single parent of one or more children. In each state of life, we discover, there awaits a rich variety of opportunities.

In an evolving universe, one sees that a choice of a state in life is merely *one step in identifying one's personal life purpose.*

For example, suppose a young man in your neighborhood chooses to become a priest in the Roman Catholic Church. What would be his unique purpose in the Spirit's evolving plan? One has only to survey a hundred different priests to discover that, although each of them is truly a priest, each has a different life purpose. Some might be dedicated to teaching theology while others may be dedicated to scientific research, hospital administration, exploring ancient scriptural documents, foreign missionary work, or managing the finances of a diocese. Some priests may dedicate their days to working for social justice, editing magazines, counseling the troubled, or pastoring parish communities. Some priests even become physicians, psychiatrists, public officials, musicians, artists, or television personalities. Even after his ordination to the priesthood, your young neighbor has still to find his unique life purpose in the divine plan.

There is just as much variety in life purpose among those who choose to marry or remain single. *Your state in life is not the same as your unique purpose in the divine plan.*

CHAPTER 4

THE MOST GENERAL
LAW OF EVOLUTION

The Jesuit priest-scientist, Father Pierre Teilhard de Chardin, discovered a general law of evolution, a law that governs all evolutionary processes.

As stated earlier, according to science, creation started as a Big Bang. Scientists tell us that in the first moments of space/time there were only photons of light and elementary particles—such as electrons, protons, and neutrons—exploding outward in all directions. Scientists estimate, with some degree of consensus, that the universe is about 13.75 billion Earth-years old. Our planet Earth, however, is only a little more than four billion years old.

The point is that, during those thirteen-plus billion years, creation has transformed itself from its primitive state of exploding elementary (subatomic) particles into a universe of billions of galaxies, each with billions of stars, and each star with planets swirling about it. Our planet, which probably started as a spinning ball of molten metal, is now a planet teeming with more than seven billion conscious human beings who have developed highly complex civilizations.

How did creation, starting as simple elementary particles, learn to turn these particles into highly intelligent, complex human organisms, complete with minds and aspirations?

What might be the law that governed or guided that evolutionary process from inert particles to complex conscious organisms?

According to Teilhard, the most general law of evolution may be described as *Attraction-Connection-Complexity-Consciousness*. In other words, attraction, as the most basic force in creation, leads to connections. Connections in turn produce complexity. And increasing complexity requires increasing consciousness to comprehend and integrate it.

As a very simple example, consider Avery, who found herself attracted to playing a musical instrument: the flute. That attraction leads her to form connections with a flute teacher and the school band. These new connections make her life more complex. She has to spend more time each day practicing her instrument; she is required to perform more difficult and complicated music; she has to deal with other personality types in the school band; she has to fit band rehearsals and performances into her already busy schedule. All this new complexity demands that she develop new levels of consciousness, learn to read the complex language of written music, master musical scales on her instrument, develop new dexterity of fingers and breath control, grasp new musical ideas and concepts, and become an integral part of the band. She must now not simply play notes on her flute, but she must also feel and hear her part as a sound that blends with fifty other instrumental sounds to produce one grand sound through every moment of the performance. To do all that requires developing an expanded consciousness, a way of thinking that she didn't possess before she first chose the flute. In other words, the young flutist's evolving life in music is following this evolutionary law, from attraction to connection to complexity to new consciousness. And the evolutionary process never stops, as she graduates from the school band to the symphony orchestra, and beyond.

According to Teilhard, the loving, divine, creative Spirit placed this *Law of Attraction-Connection-Complexity-Consciousness* not only into every human being but also into every elementary particle at the Big Bang, and this law has been driving the evolutionary process ever since. Over hundreds of millions of years, our planet, living in that divine milieu of Love, proceeded to become more and more complex. That same evolutionary law also keeps driving living forms to develop higher, more complex, and more conscious ways of being and interacting. Today, the same divine Spirit embodied in and expressed through that law is still pushing us forward and upward, little by little, each day, and each year. While the divine project sometimes appears to stall or to fall backward a few steps, the positive force of divine grace is inexorable. Scientists help us to see how that forward movement, starting from the Big Bang, appears unstoppable.

After the Big Bang, as elementary particles found themselves attracted to each other, they began to make connections and gave rise to atoms of different gases, minerals, and metals and all the other elements of the chemical table.

The basic inbuilt drive to attraction and connection placed in every particle in the first moment of creation never stopped pushing forward toward consciousness. But this required a long evolutionary process.

In Earth's evolution, the stages of attraction and connection began the process. Atoms of different chemical elements were attracted to join to form molecules. Thus, the sodium-and-chlorine connection emerged as a molecule of ordinary table salt; hydrogen and oxygen joined to make molecules of water. In a similar way, many combinations of molecules eventually formed thousands of different molecular structures. As eons of time passed, the structures—or connections—being formed became more and more complex.

Inorganic compounds led to organic compounds. Eventually, the complexity became so great that the evolutionary law led to the emergence of the first cell, the first life form.

The same evolutionary law continued to push and steer every cell through attraction and connection in the drive toward complexity and consciousness. Single-celled organisms led to multicellular organisms.

These new multicellular connections were able to do things that none of their elements could do by themselves. For example, multicellular organisms typically contain specialized cells that team together to enable the organism to eat and digest, to move about, to sense the presence of other organisms, to respond to external stimuli, and to reproduce—all of the specialized cells working cooperatively for the survival and growth of the larger multicellular organism.

Such new abilities and qualities that emerged through connection—such as movement, digestion, and cooperation—are called *emergent properties*, emergent because they weren't present before the new connection was made and only emerged because of the new connection.

In time, other evolving organisms developed more complex emergent properties of sensation (touch, smell, taste, sight, and hearing). In turn, the primitive brain, with its emergent ability to perceive and remember, emerged in fish and reptiles, and finally awareness and consciousness emerged in animals and humans.

Animals and humans have been developing awareness and consciousness for millions of years. Animals developed both family and social lives. Humans continued forward and developed language, symbolism, self-reflection, social structures, and culture.

The same evolutionary Law of Attraction-Connection-Complexity-Consciousness that pushed Avery to become a concert musician is still at work in individuals and in groups of humans, creating teams and groups, villages and cities. This driving force is helping reshape human civilizations by reenvisioning and remaking our planet Earth. The divine Spirit continues to work, individually and collectively within us and around us, making things more complex and challenging humans to develop higher stages of consciousness.

For example, consider the evolution of communication. For

tens of thousands of years, humans had only verbal communication. Eventually, less than five thousand years ago, we learned to
write. For millennia, writing by hand—and copying by hand—
was the only way to communicate other than verbally and to
preserve the written word. Only in the fifteenth century was the
printing press invented, allowing writings to be easily dupli-
cated, distributed, and shared.

We had to wait until the late nineteenth century before we
could use wires to communicate—by telegraph and telephone.
With Marconi we took the next step and began to communicate
wirelessly using radio signals. In the twentieth century, we began
to enjoy television and film, and now in the new century "smart
phones" emerge. Using these devices, with their ever-growing
complexity and convenience, today we can communicate not only
with other persons throughout the world almost instantly, but we
also have access to global tracking systems and myriad sources of
information and suggestions. With available smart phone apps,
we can instantly, from anywhere in the world, communicate and
transact business with banks, stores, schools, churches, civic
organizations, governments, worldwide news sources, book and
music publishers, clubs, organizations, and sports teams.

On the horizon, smart phone apps will soon be able to continually monitor many dimensions of our personal health, avoid
expensive exams that currently can only be done in hospitals or
clinics, and enable us to participate in doctor visits by dialing in
from our own homes, automobiles, or wherever we happen to be.

When the first automobiles rolled off the assembly lines at
the original Ford Motor plant, its engine assembly was simple
enough that a Model T's owner could carry out most of the ser-
vicing required to keep the car running. Today's autos possess a
complexity of parts and capacities, many of which are computer
driven. The average owners have little or no idea how to fix their
own vehicles.

But not all inventions come to us without liabilities. For
example, complexity in automobiles continues to evolve, but

clearly its evolution is still incomplete, especially since gasoline-burning vehicles remain a major source of pollution and ecological damage. The challenges remain.

The divine plan, too, is still incomplete. It is still evolving. We are not yet primarily a planet of peace and love. Like today's vehicles, we humans still pollute the planet with greed, violence, selfishness, and the desire for power and domination.

CHAPTER 5

THE EVOLUTIONARY LAW AS A LAW OF LOVE

The evolutionary Law of Attraction-Connection-Complexity-Consciousness may sound a bit abstract and intellectual to the religious mind. Yet, in nearly all religions the deity is considered to be pure, infinite intelligence and wisdom. In many traditions, divinity is also considered to have the nature of "personhood" and thus to have a "name." In these traditions, God is also viewed as interpersonal and relational, wishing to share the divine life of pure Love with each individual in the human family. How does a God whose name is Love relate to this evolutionary law?

The answer is quite simple. *The evolutionary law is also a law of love.*

Consider human relationships. All loving human relationships in their beginning and into their development follow the evolutionary Law of Attraction-Connection-Complexity-Consciousness. Whether it's a friendship, a marriage, or a commitment to a sports team, a healthy human relationship begins with mutual attraction and moves to connection; the connection brings complexity into each partner's life, if only in dealing with different personalities, and each one must expand consciousness—learning to think on behalf of the relationship or team—in order for the relationship or team to find and realize its true purpose for existing.

WHY DID GOD MAKE ME?

You may never have thought about it, but the most fundamental laws of physics that govern the material world, such as gravity and electromagnetism, and the rest, are Laws of Attraction and Connection. Although the forces of gravity and electromagnetism don't look like "love" as we think of it, these are inert matter's way of showing its drive to relatedness and togetherness. They are manifesting attraction, connection, and growing complexity. With more obvious expressions of attraction and connection, such as among animals and humans, the element of loving becomes much more recognizable to us.

And at the highest levels of complexity and consciousness among human beings, one can envision a powerful universal, all-encompassing love as the final evolutionary stage—one immense, peaceful, loving union of all things and persons.

What is significant for us humans living today is that *this same evolutionary law, at work since the Big Bang, forms the source of each person's own life purpose—as well as the human need to have a life purpose.*

We are all called to live a life that promotes Attraction-Connection-Complexity-Consciousness. So whether you are a research physicist, CEO of a Fortune 500 company, a flutist in a symphony orchestra, a busy parent, a checker at your local supermarket, or a homeless person, the focus or direction of your life purpose is measured by how well it fulfills and promotes the Law of Attraction-Connection-Complexity-Consciousness.

You are called to make a positive difference in your world, to promote the evolutionary divine project. Your purpose will always be linked to that fundamental law governing all evolutionary processes, the Law of Attraction-Connection-Complexity-Consciousness, the law that is ultimately the Law of Love.

Your life purpose is meant to make a contribution to that divine plan—perhaps many contributions—by observing the evolutionary law in your everyday life: to love.

You are called to love using any and all of the many ways of expressing love—listening and understanding, affirming, and supporting, displaying acts of kindness and sharing, showing compassion and forgiveness, working for justice and equality, caring for each other and building relationships, creating beauty in nature and through art and music, protecting Earth and animal life, teaching and coaching, counseling and directing, healing and consoling, hugging and kissing, believing in and hoping, trusting and encouraging, providing entertainment and laughter, inventing ways of bringing people together and making advances in human living, breaking boundaries of knowledge and science.

All these and many more expressions of loving foster the evolutionary law and help nudge the Spirit's work forward and upward.

CHAPTER 6

PRACTICING THE EVOLUTIONARY LAW IN YOUR EVERYDAY LIFE

No matter how exalted or significant your life purpose may seem to be, you will always be expected to practice daily these four elements or forces—attraction, connection, complexity, and consciousness—in all your relationships and activities. Your daily practice of these four forces will also enhance your success in achieving your personal contributions to the divine plan. Let's look at each element separately.

Attraction

It never hurts to have an approachable physical appearance, to be well groomed, clean, and neat. You are not required to look glamorous or to dress in formal clothes, except in certain avenues of employment or at important social events.

What makes you attractive and approachable, even more important than wearing trendy clothing, is what some people call your demeanor, that is, your relaxed posture, your welcoming smile, and your kind tone of voice as you interact with others. People can be turned off easily by a grimace or a gruff voice. Remember, attraction's purpose is to make—or maintain—a connection. Attraction is important because it is meant to lead to connections. Making yourself attractive for its own sake is less important than how it strengthens your ability to connect.

You might agree that what makes persons most attractive is when they listen to you attentively and respectfully. Along with that, attitudes such as friendliness, kindness, thoughtfulness, graciousness, courtesy, and the like are bound to make you more approachable.

No matter whether you are speaking to the holiest person or the worst sinner, you are speaking to someone who, like you, has a divine purpose to fulfill on Earth. Your purpose is to connect with each one as positively as possible. It may take a bit of practice, but remember, "Practice makes perfect."

Some attitudes that do not make a person attractive include being critical, cynical, pessimistic, bossy, intrusive, closed minded, ungrateful, self-centered, manipulative, or one who likes to blame or make fun of others. These attitudes do not typically lead to healthy and productive connections.

Attraction has many dimensions. People can be not only physically attractive, but also intellectually, emotionally, socially, and spiritually attractive. We can develop attractiveness in all of those dimensions.

Connection

Connections are best made when two people are attracted to each other, which is why attraction is the first stage of the evolutionary law. If there is little or no attraction between two people, there is less likelihood of a successful connection being made, which means a potential connection being lost.

The drive to be attractive is inherent in all of creation, even in inert matter. So you may also be attracted to other things like animals, nature, science, music, sports, languages, art, writing, drawing, or other fields of interest.

Notice that the most fundamental laws of physics are Laws

of Attraction and Connection—gravity, magnetism, and the various forces that hold atoms and their nuclei together. Even the most fundamental single-celled organisms tend to be attracted to each other and to form colonies.

When connections are made, new unities are formed. From these unities arise emergent properties, that is, the union (relationship, team, family, group, committee, community) often possesses abilities that none of the individual members possess on their own. An orchestra can perform a symphony, but a single violin player cannot. A basketball team can win a game, but a single player cannot. We may like to imagine that Thomas Edison made all his inventions working in solitude in his laboratory; the fact is he had teams of people working with him.

You can be sure that your life purpose will typically be somehow relational or involve groups or teams of people, because the divine project always involves building loving relationships.

How do people nurture connections once those connections are made? They begin to recognize the relationship itself as something meaningful and potentially important for each member's purpose in life. Groups, whether sports teams, families, or business, should plan to do things together, to have shared projects and fun times. Physical presence helps strengthen connections. You can cooperate and learn to appreciate and enjoy the healthy and good things that your friend or partner enjoys; or at least you shouldn't deprive them of doing what they enjoy. Also, you can discourage unhealthy or dangerous activities or habits others may have; this is a form of caring connection as well.

In addition you can offer support and affirm others. You should show gratitude and appreciation and always be ready to forgive. You should try to put the best interpretation on what others say or do. Watching out for others is important too. Sharing what you have with others, including your time, your talents, your interests, your experience, and your connections is invaluable.

You will notice that, no matter what your personal life purpose may be, you can never absolve yourself from being a good friend and caring for the poor, the lonely, the dejected, the marginalized, the forgotten, the disabled, the addicted, and everyone else in need who crosses your life path. Jesus didn't cure individuals from mental or physical illness just to prove that he was a healer. Jesus healed because he wanted all people to be whole. When people are whole, they can make their contributions better and more easily because they are healthy and not in pain. Even while we experience illness, we can inspire and love others.

Complexity

Whenever you form connections with others through friendship, marriage, work, school, hobbies, sports, politics, or religion, it invariably complexifies your life.

When you enter upon a shared project with others, it will further complexify your life. Whenever students join a sports team, a drama group, a chess club, a science club, or the school orchestra, they must develop new skills, build new relationships, learn to cooperate and deal with different personalities.

Although most people would like to simplify their lives, the real positive evolutionary strategy is to complexify. What complexity forces people to do—this is divine evolutionary strategy at work—is to reach mentally for some unifying principle (or process or system) that operates at a higher level than the level you are on currently, a new level that integrates all the complex issues of a lower level.

The smart phone is a good example of a unifying principle or system, because it integrates a number of tasks at a lower level into one piece of electronic equipment operating at a higher level. The smart phone provides not only a telephone but also a camera, a map, an encyclopedia, an amusement center, a restaurant guide, a music sound system, the ability to do instant banking, and hundreds of other applications. Avery, the flute player mentioned in chapter 4, uses a special app on her smart phone for tuning her musical instrument to ensure that the flute is in pitch with the international musical standard. The smart phone is very complex, yet simple in its organizational abilities. When used consciously and wisely, it allows people to be more fully themselves. As a rule, complexity forces us to be more conscious. If we fail to become adequately conscious in dealing with growing complexity, we can be overwhelmed by it or easily become totally absorbed in the new technology and become its slave.

Next to relationships, education is perhaps the greatest and widest source for nurturing complexity. Learning something new challenges us to integrate into our thinking more and more facts, ideas, theories, processes, and skills. It also gives birth to new levels of consciousness.

Consciousness

It is sometimes hard to believe that the same creation that started off with a universe full of only photons and elementary particles has evolved to produce such a complex, emergent property as self-reflective human consciousness. Moreover, there is no reason to believe that the self-reflective consciousness we enjoy today is the highest degree of consciousness there is to attain.

As daily news reports confirm, we have yet to learn how to live as a human community without declaring war on each other and killing thousands of men, women, and children; or standing by while immense populations of fellow human beings live lives of continual poverty and hunger. We still need to outgrow our apparent habits of worshiping money, power, and domination over others, or contentedly living with a visual entertainment diet, much of it displaying gratuitous violence and sex.

Yes, we still have a long way to go before we humans develop a level of consciousness that can create and maintain our planet as one great loving community.

There are thousands of different ways to begin making the world a better place, and each of us is needed to accomplish our part in it, or at least help take us to the next stage of consciousness. Each of us is called to use attraction, connection, complexity, and consciousness to keep us moving forward and upward.

Most of the behaviors described under these four headings are required daily of everyone seeking to make divinity's grand plan happen. There is nothing unique about these requirements. However, there is still the call to identify one's life purpose, to become more conscious of the unique project or projects you will be involved in during your lifetime.

The process of reflecting on the big picture of your life and discovering how it reveals your unique life purpose is described in the following chapters. Discovering and formulating that life purpose may be one of the most important and deeply satisfying tasks you'll ever do.

An Important Note

It is possible that the major contribution to the divine project you are called to make (1) may not be accomplished in your lifetime and/or (2) may not be the result you planned or hoped for, but is a result that in the grand plan is important.

The Hebrew patriarch Abraham was promised that his descendants would be as numerous as the stars in the sky, yet when he died, he had only one child by his wife, Sarah. Nevertheless, he held on to the promise with strong hope. Most of the founders of great movements—to eradicate slavery, to provide human rights to all children, to struggle for equal rights for women—never lived to see their dreams fulfilled, but that didn't stop them from pursuing those dreams with hope.

In one of his books, the Trappist monk Basil Pennington reflected on the grand vocation and task given to Jesus during his life on Earth. The wise monk summed up Jesus's life and mission in the following way as an encouragement to those who may have been given tasks that they cannot complete in their lifetimes:

> We should not let the magnitude of the task deter us from doing our little bit. One ripple can become a wave. He who is our Master, the Teacher of the Way, began with a few poor neighbors, not the brightest. But he gave them what he had as best he could—it was a discouraging experience that evoked salty tears of disappointment—and then he called upon the Father to send the Spirit. And it went on from there.[1]

Jesus once likened the kingdom of God to a mustard seed. It is the smallest of all seeds, yet it grows into a large bush. It takes much faith to sow the seeds of our own seemingly ordinary contributions and to trust that somehow they will make a difference, perhaps not in our lifetime, but with the work of others—as happened to Jesus.

Yet, every one of our small efforts does make a difference. We are all sowers of mustard seeds, possessing within ourselves the ability to accomplish things that move the divine project forward. The divine Spirit within us is always encouraging and inspiring us to do so. Everyone is able to contribute to building the kingdom of God here on Earth. The sum of all the individual contributions shared enriches the lives of all.

Robert F. Kennedy, who was assassinated in 1968 while running for the presidency of the United States, understood this idea of starting important work that will be carried forward by others. "Each of us can work to change a small portion of events," he said, "and in the total of all those deeds will be written the history of this generation."[2]

NOTES

1. M. Basil Pennington, OSCO, *Centering Prayer: Renewing an Ancient Christian Prayer Form.* New York: Doubleday, 1980, 249–50.

2. Robert F. Kennedy, Day of Affirmation address delivered at the University of Capetown, South Africa, June 6, 1966.

PART II

A
STEP-BY-STEP
PROCESS

CHAPTER 7

FORMULATING YOUR LIFE PURPOSE

In the following chapters, you are invited to work through a number of steps, thoughtfully and prayerfully, in a formal reflective program to identify—or confirm—your personal life purpose. It is a step-by-step discernment process for helping you find your place and role in today's evolving world. It is designed to help you (1) see how far you have come, (2) how you have been led today, (3) what were—and are—the strongest influences (internal and external) guiding you, and (4) who you are being called to become.

When you have completed this process, you should be able to formulate your life purpose, at least tentatively, in a single sentence.

Here are some examples of such sentences:

- *I choose to live as an instrument of God's love and healing in the world.*
- *I am called to show people how to raise their consciousness.*
- *I wish to show students how to enjoy mathematics and science.*
- *I am committed to working in sports with young people, to teach them how to be good team players.*
- *I wish to encourage artists to keep working and I help find venues for them to display their talents.*

41

- I want to help create laws that protect the environment.
- I want to help people be more aware of environmental needs.
- I'm meant to be a connector. I find ways to bring together people who need to meet and influence each other.
- I feel I am called to help people find ways to inner peace.
- I want to show people simple ways to bring up happy, healthy, and productive children.
- I want to help people deal with physical pain without relying completely on drugs.
- I believe I am called by God to care for animals.
- I want to show others who have the same disease as I have that they can still make a positive difference in the world.
- I wish to help people and groups become more compassionate and considerate whenever it would make the world healthier.
- I am called to help people realize that God has work for them to do—and to help them look for it.
- I feel that I am called to live my life focused on researching human history.

We will be using the evolutionary Law of Attraction-Connection-Complexity-Consciousness, first identified and developed by the Jesuit priest-scientist Pierre Teilhard de Chardin, as a helpful guide for finding and carrying out your personal divine purpose in life. We use this law because, as Teilhard realized, it is the Law of Love that the divine Spirit implanted in every elementary particle of creation—as well as in you.

This law is the inner force governing and guiding the evolution of everything in the universe. It is the law that will bring the divine project to its successful completion. And it will serve as a guide in the following chapters for you to recognize and identify your personal life purpose within that divine plan for creation. We believe you can never go wrong following the Law of Attraction-Connection-Complexity-Consciousness.

All of the personal life purposes listed previously involve attraction and connection, of course, but they also involve increased complexity and the challenge to stretch consciousness in self and others.

For example, a nurse practitioner who sees herself as an instrument of God's love and healing will want to continue learning new methods of healing, each of which will add complexity to the information and skills she currently possesses. It will also require her to raise her consciousness to a higher level in order to integrate new knowledge and skills into her current way of practicing her healing art.

A teacher who wants to show his students "how to love mathematics" faces a challenge with each new class of students who come into his classroom. He must find individual ways that help make math attractive for the different personalities of his students. This complexifies his teaching task, because he must do much more to achieve his purpose than simply present the assigned class material to his students each day. He needs to tap into each student's special interests and show how math can enhance what that student wants to become. In developing such interest-inducing approaches, he expands his consciousness and his capabilities for achieving his life purpose.

Just as this divine law will almost always prove useful for everyone in making decisions and choices—everyday ones as well as major ones—it also offers a clear guide for identifying how you are called uniquely to contribute to the divine project during your lifetime on Earth.

As you work through this process, you will begin to clarify your personal life purpose, and you, with a bit of divine grace and inspiration, may be able to formulate a statement like those mentioned that is uniquely yours.

CHAPTER 8

THE FIRST ATTRACTION QUESTION

The reflective process at this first stage asks you to ponder prayerfully three general questions related to the power of attraction. The procedure presented in this and the following chapters may be one of the more important activities you will do in identifying your life purpose. To carry it out, it will be helpful to have a notebook to record the questions as well as your responses to them.

Before Each Session

Before you begin each reflective session, take a few moments to allow yourself to grow calm and, in any way you prefer, become aware of the divine Spirit's presence, within you and all around you, lovingly guiding and supporting you in this endeavor.

In this loving atmosphere, you may also wish to begin by affirming your choice to work to help renew the face of the Earth, and your gratitude for the opportunity to make your unique contribution to the great evolutionary project.

SOME SUGGESTIONS FOR BECOMING AWARE OF THE DIVINE PRESENCE

There are many, many ways to become aware that you are in the divine presence. If you have a favorite way of doing this, please use it. If you would like some help, here are a few suggestions:

- *As you grow quiet, breathing gently, imagine yourself immersed in an immense sea of divine light, surrounding you and flowing into you with each breath, filling your entire body.*

- *Using your imagination, picture Jesus (at any age you wish) standing beside you, eager to be with you, lovingly encouraging you and supporting your reflection. Gratefully acknowledge his presence.*

- *Picture your heart opening to welcome the love energy of the Holy Spirit, and ask that this divine spirit of loving wisdom fill your mind and heart in a special way during this period of prayer.*

- *With each exhalation of your breath, silently repeat a simple prayer such as "Come, Lord Jesus!" or "Abba, I know you are here!" or "Thy will be done on Earth." Do this until your mind has quieted.*

Sometimes, when you first practice becoming aware of the divine presence, it may take a few minutes to get quiet and focused. As you practice, the process becomes more and more familiar and happens more quickly.

THE FIRST ATTRACTION QUESTION

What are the people, places, events, activities, groups, and ideas that you find especially attractive?

Interpret the word *attractive* here in its broadest meaning. Feel free in this first question to replace *attractive* with related adjectives, like *interesting, fascinating, appealing, inspiring, exciting, curious, peaceful, meaningful,* and so on.

Then separate this general question into a series of six more specific questions, and answer each of them:

1. *What kinds of* **people** *do you prefer to spend time with?*

   These could include people in your present life whom you meet most every day, like family members, coworkers, fellow students. List also friends or acquaintances you see less frequently, people whom you have met in the past but would still enjoy being with, even people you enjoyed but who are deceased. You may include people you have never met but would like to, such as historical personalities or deeply spiritual people. They could even be fictional characters from a novel, film, or a television show. All of these would help reveal your life purpose.

2. *What kinds of* **activities** *do you most enjoy?*

   Here, list activities you enjoy, alone or with others, at home, at work, at school, at church, on teams, in clubs; traveling, recreational activities, gatherings, entertainment, educational, sporting, art, and musical events, or online activities.

3. *What kinds of* **places** *do you tend to gravitate toward?*

   Here, the focus is on specific *locations* and may include home (your room, kitchen, backyard, basement, garden, or another "at home" location), work-

47

place (a specific part of the workplace), a certain classroom, an area of a certain church, holiday locations, vacation spots, travel destinations, amusement parks, sports arenas, concert venues, friends' homes, and so on.

4. *What kinds of **events** excite you? Or calm you? Or inspire you? Or challenge you?*

Here, you might make four lists and categorize them under *exciting, calming, inspiring,* and *challenging*. Events can include anything from a noisy rock concert to a quiet conversation with a longtime friend. Or even arranging to meet someone you've heard about or someone you admire. This is a very important subquestion that deserves much reflection, because it indicates where and how you prefer to spend your energy.

5. *What kinds of **groups** would you choose to belong to?*

Here, list not only the groups you already belong to and enjoy or have belonged to and enjoyed in the past, but also groups you would like to belong to but at present do not or cannot. Such groups might include relationships that revolve around family, work, school, community, church, social, political, military, financial, intellectual, medical, scientific, art, music, sports, education, volunteer service organizations, as well as others. Perhaps you are also attracted to groups dedicated to certain values such as creativity, social justice, peacemaking, working with the poor or disabled, immigration, or many other issues.

6. *What kinds of **ideas** turn you on?*

Here, focus on what you like to think about. Many people delight in thinking about eating, drinking, sex, and ways to escape stress. While not excluding these, probe a little deeper. For example, what kinds of injustice or mistreatment of others get you angry? Think of the books you like. Do you like humor, puzzles, or mysteries? Mathematical or scientific ideas? Creative, inspiring, inventive, or new ideas—what kinds, specifically? Scientific, philosophical, or spiritual ideas? Do you like devising strategies? Planning? Organizing? Calculating? Risk taking? Debating? Again, stay with this exploratory process. Don't rush it.

All of these questions are part of the First Attraction Question. If the divine Spirit is working through you, it will certainly happen through some form of attraction. Attraction is the first and primary energy working upon you, focusing your attention, getting you to take notice, releasing your energy, getting you to take action. The forces of attraction never stop working.

REFLECTIVE PROCESS

In dealing with each of the breakdown questions, there are four steps or stages of reflection.

STEP ONE

Take each of the breakdown questions, one by one. Under each question, list your response. Try to *list at least three or four responses to each question.*

For example, Lou answered the question *What activities do you most enjoy?* He listed *music, mathematics, writing, using the computer,* and *eating.*

Using the same question, *Which activities do you most enjoy?* Pat listed *helping people, music, theater, spending time with children and close friends, walking in nature, being with animals, planting flowers,* and *kayaking.*

An Important Note

Please do not rush this attraction process, as it may be crucial to identifying your life's special purpose. Take your time working through each of the six subquestions.

You may always come back later and add more items to each of your lists. For example, Lou later recalled his delight in *reading mystery stories and watching mystery episodes on television*, as well as *going to flea markets, grocery shopping,* and *cooking*. People do not always build a complete list on their first attempt. So, leave room beneath each step of the process for additional notes or comments.

STEP TWO

After each name or item in each list, specify in writing what it is you enjoy about this person, event, activity, or idea. *What aspect or quality of each makes it attractive to you?*

For example, Lou is attracted to music. But why? He doesn't particularly enjoy listening to music; he doesn't have a portable music player; he doesn't own a record collection; he doesn't listen to music while driving. So what is it about music he finds attractive? He likes to *perform and create music*. He plays trumpet and French horn in several community bands. He also loves to compose and orchestrate music, and he can lose himself for hours when he is composing musical arrangements for bands or vocal groups.

Although Pat, like Lou, is attracted to music, her attraction has an entirely different meaning for her, which is why we ask the question: *Why are you attracted to this activity?* For Lou, music offers a venue for public performance. For Pat, who does not play a musical instrument and has no desire to learn that skill, her focus is on *listening* to music because it has the ability to transport her back to a happy memory, uplift, or comfort her. Sometimes she likes to use music to meditate. Other times she likes to listen to music that has rhythm and makes her want to tap her feet or just "float on it," as she puts it.

STEP THREE

What is there within your special preferences of this activity that most attracts you?

If we ask Lou what interests lie beneath his music preferences for performance and orchestration, he might say, "I love to perform music because it makes people happy. And I love composing and arranging because I love the structure, the symmetry, the order of music, and that I can create structure, symmetry, and order when I write music."

If we ask Pat the same question, she might say, "I love music for its emotional qualities, such as its ability to put me in a desirable mood, its ability to bring back fond memories of occasions when I was with people I love, and its healing qualities."

STEP FOUR

After you have done the first three steps of the process for each of the six subquestions in this category, review all of the material gathered from step 3 in each case and *look for similarities and themes.* In these themes and similarities you will begin to find key elements of your life purpose.

In Lou's case, after he went through steps 1, 2, and 3 for each of the *activities* he is attracted to, he noticed a few common themes running through his preferences, namely, his love for *communicating, structure, organizing, clarifying, simplifying,* and *creating.* These themes came up again and again as he was doing this exercise. It begins to give him some important clues about his life purpose.

First Attraction Question (Lou's Summary)

2. *What kinds of **activities** do you most enjoy?*		
Step 1	**Step 2**	**Step 3**
music	perform compose orchestrate	
mathematics	order clarity structure	*structure*
writing	organization clarity simplicity	*symmetry* *organization* *creativity*
using computers	efficient revisable	*clarity* *simplification*
cooking	control planning inventive	

First Attraction Question (Pat's Summary)

In Pat's case, after going through these same steps, she noticed a few common themes that were quite different from those Lou observed. For her, some prominent themes include *storytelling, compassion, nurturing, appreciating, healing, raising consciousness,* and *inviting creativity.* These became important clues to identifying her life purpose.

2. What kinds of **activities** do you most enjoy?		
Step 1	**Step 2**	**Step 3**
helping people	chances to love chances to get close chances to learn, teach 	 *remembering*
music, theater	emotional stimulation exploring personalities	*storytelling* *caring* *healing emotions*
time with children	intimacy sharing stories inviting consciousness learning	*loving, compassion* *affirming* *nurturing* *appreciating*
walking in nature	in touch with God loving creation	*learning*
planting flowers	helping growth nurturing	

An Important Note

Your life purpose will typically be broader than your job or profession, because the divine evolutionary process is at work at all times, not merely during workplace hours. You may choose to become a physician, an electrical engineer, a financial planner, a meteorologist, a clergyperson, an educator, a therapist, or a novelist. The occupation or position you choose to follow as a career is usually not your life purpose. It merely provides the context, the structure, in which you may fulfill your life purpose.

CHAPTER 9

THE SECOND ATTRACTION QUESTION

The Second Attraction Question is the opposite of the first. This one helps you identify what typically does *not* attract you, what you do *not* find interesting, fascinating, appealing, exciting, inspiring, curious, or meaningful.

When you are on a journey, the roads you do not take are perhaps as important in getting to your destination as the roads you do take. In finding your personal life purpose, it is important to discern the paths you are *not* being attracted to follow, because they help clarify the paths you were meant to follow.

The question for reflection here is:

What are some of the people, places, events, activities, groups, and ideas that you find much less attractive?

Or more specifically:

1. What kinds of **people** do you prefer to stay away from?
   Here, you may begin by reviewing the people clos-est to you *presently* whom you prefer to stay away from, whom you encounter in your family, your work-place, your school, your church, your neighborhood, or among your acquaintances. Then, look at the people you have avoided or wished to avoid *in your*

past—recently, a few years ago, in your youth, your childhood. Note also people in the news you would not want to deal with, characters or personalities on television whom you feel an aversion toward.

2. *What **activities** would you prefer to avoid?*

Think of the contexts where you would say, "I don't want to do that," "I'd rather not join you in that," "It's not my thing," or something similar. These are the kinds of activities to list here. Are there certain kinds of films or television shows you would avoid? Are there activities at home, at work, school, or church you prefer to avoid? Are there activities associated with entertainment or vacations you would avoid?

3. *What kinds of **places** do you prefer not to frequent?*

Here, you could list locations, specific or general, that you would avoid whenever possible. These places might be homes of certain family members, shopping malls or specific shops, areas in your workplace, places that have bad memories connected with them, or places that feel scary, threatening, repugnant, or emotionally uncomfortable.

4. *What kinds of **events** sadden you? Or bore you? Or discourage you?*

Here, it is the event rather than the location that you prefer not to attend, for whatever reason. In addition to the three negative emotional responses suggested, some events can be frightening, disgusting, demeaning, offensive, or painful. You may find some of these at your workplace or in the community. Other events or displays, perhaps reported by the media, that turn you off may happen at the local, state, national, or world level. After each event, note the negative emotion that the event typically engenders in you.

5. *What kinds of **groups** would you choose not to join?*
Such groups may be related to your family, your workplace, your church, your community. These groups may be clubs or sports groups; political, religious, or intellectual organizations; artistic or entertainment related. Think of all the different groups that people you know belong to, and decide whether—all other things being equal—you would choose to belong to any of them.

6. *What kinds of **ideas** turn you off?*
You may find some help making this list by reviewing the list of ideas in the First Attraction Question that turned you on, and doing comparisons. What kinds of ideas do you find repugnant, disgusting, frightening, saddening, threatening, or angering?

In dealing with each question, as previously, there are four steps or stages of reflection.

STEP ONE

List at least three or four responses to each question.

For example, Lou took the question, *What kinds of places do you prefer not to frequent?* He listed a number of places he does not like to frequent, or at least he does not enjoy certain aspects of: *amusement parks, rock concerts, swimming in the ocean, camping.*

In response to the same question, Pat listed not liking *long lectures and sermons (especially boring ones), noisy cafeterias, loud places in general, war movies, violence and gratuitous sex in films, many online seminars, reading about people hurting others or taking advantage of them for the sake of their own power or domination.*

STEP TWO

What aspect or quality of each makes it unattractive to you?

Lou commented that most amusement parks had rides that were too dangerous, while other rides that he might enjoy usually had long waiting lines. Rock concerts were too noisy, had too many people, many of whom were drunk or drugged. Swimming in the ocean felt too dangerous, and so did camping. In general, he felt that a person had little control over nature. Knowing his dislike for danger and unpredictable reactions of people, he probably could also have agreed with Pat in finding watching violence and gratuitous sex in films unattractive.

Pat observed that many of the activities she listed as unlikable—long lectures, noisy places, and online seminars—were those that offer little or no personal face-to-face interaction. War movies and violent films promote the very opposite reaction of the healing and compassionate help to which she is committed. She feels angry and helpless to hear about people willfully harming or taking advantage of others when she has no way of stopping it or righting the injustice.

STEP THREE

What especially in this activity is most unappealing to you?

Lou said that in the amusement park, the ocean, and camping he had little control over the dangers present. Once he was strapped into a roller coaster or swimming in the ocean or camping, he felt he had little chance to avoid imminent danger. At rock concerts, the mob mentality often took over; again he felt unsafe and out of control.

For Pat, the themes of a lack of face-to-face interaction, the presence of injustice, and the promotion of the values of violence are "jarring to my soul."

STEP FOUR

Look for similarities and themes.

Avoiding dangers that were out of his *control* was a common theme in Lou's dislikes. He prefers *safety* and *efficiency* (not wasting time).'

Face-to-face interaction, healing, and promoting compassion surfaced as some of Pat's major themes.

Here is Lou's summary for the subquestion *What kinds of places do you prefer not to frequent?*

Second Attraction Question (Lou's Summary)

3. What kinds of **places** do you prefer **not** to frequent?		
Step 1	Step 2	Step 3
amusement parks	dangerous rides long waiting lines	
rock concerts	too noisy crowds drunks/druggies	*efficiency* *control* *quiet*
swimming in ocean	too dangerous little control	*safety*
camping	too dangerous little control annoying bugs	

Second Attraction Question (Pat's Summary)

3. *What kinds of **places** do you prefer **not** to frequent?*		
Step 1	**Step 2**	**Step 3**
long lectures	boring too intellectual *quiet*	
noisy places	hate loud noise confusing	*gentleness* *healing* *compassion*
online seminars	too impersonal no face-to-face	*peace* *helping*
violent films	upsetting encourage anger	

NOTE

1. Some experts have observed that the qualities listed in a person's step 4 may also reveal a need to develop the reciprocal unwelcome quality. For instance, although Lou likes efficiency and not wasting time, it may also indicate his need to develop the quality of patience. His preference for safety and being in control may also indicate his need to develop the qualities of courage and risk taking. It will be helpful to revisit this insight during reflections on Complexity.

CHAPTER 10

THE THIRD ATTRACTION QUESTION

The Third Attraction Question is not focused on what you find attractive in others, but what others find attractive about you. In this regard, there is no need to look for negative comments when searching for your life purpose. Your purpose will typically manifest through your better qualities. The basic question here is:

What is there about you that attracts people to you?

To help answer that basic question, look for positive responses to the following:

- *What do people affirm about you?*
- *What nice things do they say directly to you?*
- *What affirming comments do people make to others about you?*

In addition to recording what others say about you, it is also revealing to watch how people treat you. Again, focus on the positive responses.[1]

If you can't answer the three questions by reflecting on your own experience, then ask your friends:

- *What is it about me that you like?*
- *Why do you like to spend time with me?*
- *What are the things you think I do best?*

When Lou asked his friends, *"What is it about me that you like?,"* they said things like "You know a lot of interesting things." "You are easy and fun to be with." "You can be quiet, not like people who always need to be talking."

When Pat asked the same question of her friends, they said things like "You are comforting to be with." "I'm never afraid to tell you anything, no matter how embarrassing." "You always say nice things." "You inspire me to hang in there." "You are like a good mother."

Summarize what you have learned about yourself from this Third Attraction Question.

For example, Lou realized that it was his interesting ideas that attracted people to him, as well as his sense of humor and his ability to be quiet and listen.

Pat evoked deep trust in others by her caring, protectiveness, and affirming nature.

This Third Attraction Question will lead beyond attraction to the next stage of connection.

Summary of Attraction

It is assumed that you have been writing your replies and responses to these questions and subquestions in your notebook and that by now you have many pages to review and summarize.

Many people find it helpful as they review their journals to highlight or underline important words or themes.

The attraction process of reflection should greatly help you begin to zero in on the *people, places, events, activities, groups, and ideas that will help reveal your primary life purpose.*

LOU'S NOTEBOOK SUMMARY

As I worked through the three attraction questions, it became clear that whatever purpose God had for me, it would include work that involved organizing, clarifying, simplifying, and creating. That work had to blend in with my love for efficiency, control, quiet, and safety, which indicated that my work would most likely be with the written or spoken word (or in musical notation).

In reading over Pat's responses, I realized that, although I might make a good teacher or lecturer, I would never make a good therapist, since working with people's emotional problems was as scary to me as trying to swim against an ocean current.

In reviewing the Third Attraction Question, people noticed that I was open to new ideas and that I had plenty of new ideas to share. I could be quiet and a good listener. I also noticed that when people asked me to explain some complex idea that was confusing to them, I could represent it to them in simple terms and with examples, so that they could understand it.

When someone described a problem to me, I could usually see the elements of the problem and how the elements related to each other. Asking the person a few well-placed questions, I could usually restructure or reorganize in my own mind the problem they described. Then I could re-describe it to them so they could make more sense of the situation.

When I read over Pat's responses, I realized that the problems I deal well with are mostly intellectual ones, not emotional ones like hers and I certainly couldn't do my intellectual restructuring in the very heat of the strong emotions as she does in therapeutic situations.

PAT'S NOTEBOOK SUMMARY

I have known for a long time what my personal purpose in life is. I express it as living my life *as an instrument of God's love and healing in the world*. I can remember feeling this call even as a young girl doing babysitting. I have always felt full of love for others. I remember feeling my purpose as a young step-mother, and then later as a mother of my three daughters. I remember feeling it as a teacher and tutor of young children. I have known it most clearly as a therapist where my role is to bring both love and healing to my clients or comfort and peace to the sick and dying.

In doing the First Attraction Questions, my sense of purpose was confirmed when I listed favorite activities like *helping people, spending time with children and close friends, walking in nature, being with animals*, and *planting flowers*. And the reasons I liked these activities was because they fostered *intimacy, personal interaction, relationships, beauty, nature, healing*, and *storytelling*.

The Second Attraction Question reminded me how much, as a gentle person, I hate violence and noise as well as anything that is jarring to my soul, since I am all about seeking peace, love, and healing. I relearned that I prefer personal face-to-face interaction rather than impersonal activity like computer work.

When reflecting on the Third Attraction Question and the things people say about me, I recalled their many expressions of love and trust, their knowledge that I would always try to guide or affirm them, see the best in them, and never consciously hurt them with my words or comments. I want to use my ability to be compassionate and encourage compassion in others.

This exercise confirmed that my personal purpose in life is to be a loving and healing force in the world and that I would do it mostly through personal interactions, especially with those who felt unloved and needed comfort and healing.

Expressing Gratitude for Divine Guidance

Throughout this process, you will undoubtedly experience insights that relate to your unique purpose. It is important that you express gratitude for the divine guidance you are receiving at each step along the way. Sometimes your expression of gratitude may be spontaneous, as when an insight surprises and delights you. And, at the end of each reflection period, we recommend you take a few moments to formulate a personal prayer of thanks to the loving presence that is guiding you.

NOTE

1. If people tend to avoid you, you may need to work on your own attractiveness and ability to make connections with people.

CHAPTER 11

HOW TO USE CONNECTION TO HELP FIND YOUR LIFE PURPOSE

Attraction leads to connection, but the evolutionary move to connection is more than the simple act of coming together that attraction facilitates. Connections have a life of their own. In the earliest times of the universe, atoms of hydrogen and helium experienced an attraction to each other. These two inert gases had no idea why they were coming together and joining. However, their connection, with a life of its own, generated units of tremendous energy and light that we call stars. Stars, like our Sun, are fundamentally the product of the interaction between hydrogen and helium.

Relationships, too, are human connections made up not merely of the partners and their individual actions. More important, connections are better described as the product of the partners' *interactions*, that is, what goes on between the partners when they are together. Connection focuses on how people in relationships influence one another and how a relationship itself influences each of the partners.

Connections also possess their own inner dynamics. Personal relationships, for example, have their own needs if they are to survive and thrive. In order to thrive, couples require time spent together with shared interests and projects. Friends need to spend time together to keep the friendship alive and vital. Members of a sports team need to spend time together to practice for the next game and to improve their teamwork.

Most revealing are the connections that absorb your time and interest. These are the bonds that you naturally and spontaneously nurture, simply because they bring you more joy and satisfaction than other connections or relationships. *Your most satisfying and fulfilling connections and relationships provide some of the best clues to identifying your life purpose.*

When you study your connections to other people, begin by looking at what it was that first brought you together. Usually, there is some shared interest. The link may be superficial and temporary—as in a chance meeting—or it may be deep and lasting.

Serena loves her dog. Whenever she takes her dog out for an evening walk, she invariably meets other dog walkers. One evening she met a rather elderly gentleman walking his dog. They said hello and asked about each other's dogs: "What breed? How old? Is this your first dog?" On another evening, they met again, walking their dogs. Trust had been built up during the first meeting. This time they ventured into other interests, their jobs, their hometowns, their families. A third time, they talked about their work and plans. It turned out the gentleman had a contact, whom he shared with Serena, that enabled her to find a job that she really liked, that felt right, where she could use her talents more effectively. The connection with the stranger was very temporary, but very influential.

One never knows when a connection may introduce you to your life purpose, or put you one step closer to finding it. The universe is driven to find its way toward becoming a loving unity, so the divine loving immanence brings people together to help further the grand project. That is why it is love alone, ultimately, that can unite human beings so as to help complete and fulfill them.

At a parent–teacher meeting many years ago, Patricia was talking to her eldest daughter's first grade teacher, Mrs. Chilton, who was recovering from a heart attack. She was planning on retiring from teaching. "Unless," she added, "some sweet person like you would help me in the classroom." It was Mrs. Chilton's reputation that she never had a student she couldn't teach to read. Patricia knew that if she didn't agree to help Mrs. Chilton in the classroom, her second daughter, about to enter first grade, would never experience Mrs. Chilton's wonderful teaching skills. So, both for the love of her daughter and for her own development, Patricia agreed to become Mrs. Chilton's aide. Because of that connection, Patricia went on to become a teacher, a tutor of children with learning disabilities and of children with emotional problems. From her experience, Patricia became creator of a process called "Tutoring Therapy" (using tutoring tools therapeutically) and author of the book *Building Self-Esteem in Children* that has remained in print for more than thirty years.

The connection with Mrs. Chilton was a powerfully deep and lasting one. Mrs. Chilton believed that if you helped build confidence in children they could learn what they needed to learn. Patricia developed that belief into a therapeutic principle that, when applied in almost any counseling situation with people of all ages, has proven successful.

Working in Connections

Much of the divine project will be carried out, not primarily by individuals working alone, but by people in groups and teams. Most of the various activities of the divine project need groups of people in order for them to succeed. That is why connections and relationships are so important in identifying and formulating your personal purpose.

Each year, an individual(s) is awarded a Nobel Prize for his or her scientific work. But when you talk with these winners, it becomes clear that the prize really belongs to the teams of people who worked with or under the direction of the individual prizewinner. Or consider people in the film industry, like actors and actresses, who win Oscars; notice how many people on the film team and in their families to whom they express gratitude for support and direction. Even novelists, who seem to be solitary creators, consistently thank their editors, publishers, researchers, and the scores of people who provided technical, inspirational, and professional information to make the writing accurate in its technical and informational details.

CHAPTER 12

CONNECTION QUESTIONS

Before Each Session

As you begin each reflective session, take a few moments to allow yourself to grow calm and, in any way you prefer, become aware of a divine, loving presence guiding and supporting you in this endeavor. The divine life flows through you and all around you, like the atmosphere that fills your body and surrounds you.

In this loving presence, you may also wish to affirm your desire to work to help renew the face of the Earth, and your gratitude for the opportunity to make your unique contribution to God's great evolutionary project.

The Connection Question

What are the personal connections that have helped shape your life so far?

You are invited in this chapter to make a list of these connections and to work with that list. You should be able to list at least ten or fifteen connections. You may begin making your list right now. If you need help finding ten or more, the next few paragraphs offer a number of suggestions about where to look that may trigger your memory of those who had a hand in guiding you to your life purpose.

Some of these relationships may be ones you consciously initiated and nurtured, like family and close friends; others may be relationships that were unexpected, accidental, dropped in your lap, as it were, connections that you did not initiate but came to you through the actions of others or through events that you attended. Some connections may have lasted a very short time, others were lifelong. Some connections may seem unfortunate or hurtful, others very fortunate. All of them are important.

Some of your most important connections may have been made during your childhood. Many were made during your adult years. Some connections happen late in life. Don't overlook family members. List them all.

As you progress through your life chronologically, which is what most people usually do in this process, list the names of people—connections that seem significant and influential, especially those that happened unexpectedly.

Here is the first list Lou made:

LOU'S LIST OF CONNECTIONS

Childhood & Teen Years
> Mom
> Dad
> Brother Al
> Aunt Mayme
> Richard Beckish (school chum)
> Charles Masters (trumpet teacher)
> Eva Morgan (band director)
> Neil Lally (band manager)
> Muriel Stromberg (high school teacher)

Jesuit Years
> Tom Composto, SJ (friend, musician)
> William Hill, SJ (English professor)
> Peter Esseff, SJ (friend)

Ron Lane-Smith, SJ (friend)
Edward Sheehy, SJ (friend)
Leslie Schnierer, SJ (friend, musician)
Joseph Grau, SJ (friend)
Kevin Lysaght, SJ (friend, musician)
Robert Faricy, SJ (colleague)
Robert Johann, SJ (introduced me to Teilhard)

Adult Years

Rev. Charles Curran (moral theology professor)
Thomas Collins (editor)
Rose Lucey (agent)
Sr. Trinitas Bocchini, SSND (colleague)
Mary Paolini (coauthor)
George Malhame (publisher)
Helen Bonny (coauthor)
Robert Fritz (coauthor)
Steven Halpern (coauthor)
Muriel James (coauthor)
Margaret Miller (coauthor)
Patricia Berne (wife and coauthor)
Clare Crawford-Mason (coauthor)
W. Edwards Deming (teacher)
Jefferson Vander Wolk (coauthor)

In your notes, leave plenty of space after each name for further reflection.

Work with at least ten or more of these connections who have helped shape your life so far. If you list those names now, before you read any further, bringing those individuals to your attention now will undoubtedly trigger many associations as you continue with the process. Each relationship—and your interactions in it—reveals something about your inner self and your life purpose.

NONPERSONAL CONNECTIONS

Of course, you may have encountered and developed a connection with something other than a specific individual, especially a connection that has had a significant effect on your life and your way of thinking. For example, the connection may be with an event, a group, a place, an experience, some type of information, an animal or pet, a book, a film, a documentary, a musical instrument, a tool, an automobile, or some other object or thing.

For example, certain *books* in Lou's life changed the way he thought, so he listed some of those to reflect on. His first try at a list included:

Seven Science Fiction Stories by H. G. Wells
The Divine Milieu by Pierre Teilhard de Chardin, SJ
Cat's Cradle by Kurt Vonnegut
Stranger in a Strange Land by Robert Heinlein
The Wind in the Door by Madeleine L'Engle

Answer questions like the ones following *for each individual connection on your list*. Each question assumes the connection is with a person. However, if the connection happens to be with an event, a place, an experience, some type of information, a book, or some other thing, substitute the "other thing" for "person" in each question.

- *How would you describe this person's influence on you?*
- *What did you learn from this person?*
- *If it weren't for this individual...*
  - *What choices would you not have made?*
  - *What paths would you not have taken?*
  - *What other persons would you never have met or known?*
  - *What skills would you not have?*

- *What information would you not know?*
- *What areas of your life now would you be unacquainted with?*

For example, Lou reflected on what he had learned from Kurt Vonnegut's book *Cat's Cradle*. He wrote:

I learned

- new ways to describe certain relationships;
- how to identify phony or empty relationships;
- how to identify and name the impetus that brought a relationship into connection;
- how to identify the fulcrum or axis around which a relationship revolves and evolves;
- the idea that a relationship has its own being, personality, and capacities, distinct from those of the partners;
- how partners in a relationship may maintain spirit-to-spirit connection, even when physically apart.

Lou also chose one of the people on his connection list to show as an example.

Clare Crawford-Mason

What did you learn from this person?

- loyalty
- caring
- friendship
- persistence
- hospitality
- generosity
- connection skills
- fascination with new ideas
- commitment to spiritual growth

If it weren't for her I would not have chosen to get involved in

- systems thinking;
- quality in manufacturing;
- philosophy of management;
- evolutionary mindsets;
- television documentaries;
- hospital safety.

If it weren't for her I would not have known

- W. Edwards Deming;
- Jefferson Vander Wolk;
- Lloyd Dobyns;
- Russell Ackoff.

An alternate way of dealing with this last subquestion would be to write: *If it weren't for so-and-so…* [insert the person's or other thing's name]. Then, complete that sentence with at least four or five different responses that apply to that person or thing. Do the same for each person on your list of persons or things that influenced your life.

For example, one of Lou's major interests—and purposes—in life is music performance. Many different people were significant in his musical development. One was his first trumpet teacher and music theory instructor, Mr. Masters. So, in his notebook, Lou wrote the heading:

If it weren't for Mr. Masters I would not have

- learned how to play the trumpet;
- known how to play and improvise in a musical combo;
- had the experience of playing in a 17-piece swing band;
- developed the ability to write musical notation;
- learned the art of musical transposition;

- learned the basics of music theory and chord structure;
- learned the principles of musical harmony and composition;
- had practice in arranging music for four-part voices;
- been introduced to arranging scores for marching band and orchestra.

For Pat, one of her special interests since early in her career has been tutoring children with learning disabilities. Developing skills in this area helped her a great deal in her later therapeutic and healing work with adults. One significant person in her early development was her work with Mrs. Chilton. She began with the sentence stem:

If it weren't for Mrs. Chilton I would not have

- realized how much I love teaching;
- developed the ability to turn a child's "mistake" into a learning moment;
- realized the crucial importance of building confidence and healthy self-esteem as the basis for a successful life and successful relationships;
- believed that every child could learn;
- realized that, if a child is having a difficulty learning any subject, it is the teacher's responsibility to find the way to help the child succeed, not the child's responsibility;
- developed the art of suggesting alternatives to a person in a "stuck place;"
- realized that teaching itself is a therapeutic form of healing and wholeness;
- gone on to a life dedicated to helping people succeed —at all ages;
- written a book called *Building Self-Esteem in Children.*

77

NOTE ON PEOPLE WHO ARE "CONNECTORS"

Some people in your life, called *connectors*, are there merely to ensure that you make an important connection. They form a special class of people in the grand evolutionary project. Their main life purpose is simply to make sure that two people who are destined to come together actually meet and connect. They do this kind of connecting throughout their lives. Many of us are part-time connectors—we put a few people together now and then—but we usually have a major life purpose beyond connecting. However, there are some people who are full-time connectors, whose special purpose in life is to introduce people to one another and, in the process, to point out those interests that the two strangers share in order to ensure the connection.

"UNION DIFFERENTIATES"

Teilhard also identified a significant power associated with connection, namely, that "union differentiates." Simply put, what Teilhard means is that when you form an interactive bonding, connection, relationship, or *union* with another or others, whether in a marriage, a working friendship, or a sports team, something new happens to you. In Teilhard's word, you become *differentiated*, that is, you come to a fuller realization of who you are and of what you are capable. You discover ways you are unique and different from others.

For example, if you are a member of a sports team, when interacting with that team you discover—and express—capacities you may not have known about yourself. For instance, you may discover for the first time that you can lose yourself in a team effort, you have inner resources of commitment, patience, and forgiveness for yourself and others, or that you can perform your sport at a higher level than you ever thought possible. In other words, in committing to the success of the team ("union"), you have discovered more of who you are and can become ("differentiated"). Acting within the union, you become more of your potential self. In that union, you have differentiated—or recognized and named—more of yourself than you had been aware of before you were part of that union. It is precisely the interactivity within the union that helps differentiate you and clarifies who you are.

LIST INFLUENTIAL GROUPS BY NAME

We have not emphasized your connections to teams or groups in this section of the process. However, if your connection to a group—a sports team, a musical group, a drama troupe, a science club, a volunteer organization, a research team, a shared-interest group or some other "union" where you took an active part—was important in your development, please consider reflecting on each group as a distinct influence.

Write: *If it weren't for this group [name the group] I would not have...* and write as many as five to ten endings to that sentence stem.

POWERFUL CONNECTIONS NOT WITH PERSONS

Important relationships need not always be with other human beings. An important relationship might be with a pet, a musical instrument, an automobile, a computer, a microscope, a book, a paintbrush, or something else.

As a child, Lou's nephew Alex was deeply attracted to automobiles. He absorbed everything he could about cars. Before he was sixteen and eligible for a driver's permit, he had saved enough money to buy a '57 Chevy, which he parked in the family garage. He didn't just look at it or polish it. He took it apart. Totally! Its parts were spread all over the garage floor. When he put it back together again, he repeated the entire process. He took his car totally apart twice and put it back together. This process was not an onerous chore for him, but a fascinating delight. No one asked him to do it. His love for engines and mechanics emerged from within him. It became his way of life. Before he was twenty, he had become a master mechanic. By twenty-five, he owned his own automotive garage. Within a few years, because of the quality of his service to his customers, he had earned the contract for repairing his county's entire truck fleet. He found his life's calling through his connection to vehicles.

Pat and I recently watched a teenager relating to a skateboard. In a connection with his skateboard, he discovered and developed inner qualities he would undoubtedly use throughout his life. As we sat on a park bench watching him one summer afternoon, we were truly impressed by the young man's ability to keep practicing a single act of reversing the skateboard's direction using a certain twist of his entire body. He must have failed at the trick twenty times before he succeeded for the first time. We thought he might now try learning another trick. No. He kept practicing the same trick over and over. He didn't always succeed. It must have been half an hour—and hundreds of tries—before he could finally do the trick consistently. He repeated the trick flawlessly at least ten times in succession before he kicked his skateboard up under his arm and headed for home. We doubted he would ever make the Olympic skateboarding team, but we felt sure that his perseverance at mastering a new task, here a skateboarding trick, would certainly help him in his future work and in his life purpose. His powerful connection that we observed was to his skateboard.

The famous founder of Apple computers, Steve Jobs, found that a relationship to calligraphy enriched his life and his business. Steve never finished college, but he took courses once in a while. One course he was particularly attracted to was calligraphy, the study of elegant and beautiful script and lettering. One might think that attraction to calligraphy was quite unusual for a computer geek. And it was for Jobs. He could not explain what attracted him to the course, but Jobs claimed it was one of the most important courses he ever took because in that class he fell in love with the beauty of typefaces. As a result, his Apple computers were the first to offer a variety of typefaces—or fonts—for the user to choose from. Because of Jobs's insistence on providing a variety of fonts to customers, any and every word processing program you buy today offers at least a hundred different available fonts.

REVIEW

Be sure to work through all the people on your list. Afterward, review all your notes and write down some conclusions. Some people, as they do their review of connections, like to highlight or underline phrases or qualities that seem to stand out or get repeated again and again. These are clues to clarifying your life purpose.

Most important, please take some time to express your gratitude to the divine presence that has been guiding you throughout this identification and clarification process.

Now, begin to notice how connection leads to complexity.

CHAPTER 13

COMPLEXITY
QUESTIONS

Before Each Session

As you begin each reflective session, take a few moments to allow yourself to grow calm and, in any way you prefer, become aware of a strong, yet gentle, divine presence guiding and supporting you in this procedure.

In this presence, filled with life-giving wisdom and love, you may also wish to affirm your choice to work to help renew the face of the Earth, and your gratitude for the opportunity to make your unique contribution to the great evolutionary project.

Complexity

Just as connections and relationships have a life of their own, complexity is an evolutionary factor in your life that remains very important in itself. Although specific connections and relationships often create complexity in our lives, not all people and events do—at least not directly. A normal encounter with a checkout cashier at the supermarket is not likely to bring additional complexity into your life, nor are the few words you say to the ticket seller at the cinema likely to turn your life around. However, we have known people who attended a rally, read a certain book, watched a certain film, listened to a public speaker, joined a sports team, or met by chance—and that connection changed their lives. Some people may discover their life purpose through a terrible accident.

While driving home from college, a young man sent a text to his friend, saying, "I need to quit texting because I could die in a car accident and then how would you feel...." A few seconds later, his pickup truck veered off a bridge and plunged thirty-five feet down into a ravine. After six months in the hospital, reflecting on his almost impossible survival, he realized, "I still have things to do in this world....What people have told me is the reason God didn't take me away from this Earth is because I have something special to do....And I believe what is special is that I should tell everyone not to text message and drive." The young Texan still faces additional surgeries and rehabilitation, but for the rest of his life, he promises to spread the message about the dangers of texting and driving.[1]

It is most likely that the people, places, events, and other items you listed as your special connections in the previous chapter are also connections that have brought complexity into your life—and new consciousness as well.

It's not hard to recognize complexity, though you may not typically use the word *complexity* to describe your experiences. Sometimes complexity feels like confusion, such as when it brings emotional upset to your otherwise normal life. It can feel disturbing, annoying, perhaps even frightening. What if your boss told you that you were being reassigned to a position overseas and were required to learn a foreign language within a month? What if you were told your job no longer existed and you had to learn a completely new skill in a new field? What if you as a teenager moved with your family to a new town and you had to meet and learn to get along with dozens of new classmates?

Sometimes complexity feels as complicated as a thousand-piece jigsaw puzzle, such as when you begin a new job and there are hundreds of things you must learn to perform, or a new computer software program you must learn to use, or you are asked to form and chair a committee to accomplish a number of objectives and have no idea where to begin.

The Role of Complexity

The *very large* and the *very small* are the usual classic scientific categories of measurement. The telescope is one tool we use to grasp the very large; a microscope is a tool we use to measure and view the very small.

Teilhard was the first to introduce *complexity* as a third new and significant form of measurement. What makes a system, group, or organization, such as an automobile, an extended family, or the human body, complex is not simply that it contains a multitude of elements or parts. Complexity includes the important component that these many elements interact with each other in a very systemic way.

Complexity is not to be confused with something that is complicated or difficult to understand—like statistics is for most of us. *The measure of complexity is the number and quality of the interactions of the parts.* The parts of all systems interact with one another, just as the elements of an automobile interact with one another to provide an effective and efficient vehicle of transportation, or just as the many organs and subsystems of the human body work together to sustain a living human person.

Complexity is measured by the number of parts of any system and the extent or capacity of their interactions. Thus, a human brain is more complex than the brain of a chicken. The sands on the seashore, though numerically almost infinite, are not at all high in complexity because the grains of sand do not interact very much with each other.

For Teilhard, complexity is the most important measurement in the evolutionary process and in evolutionary development. As such, complexity is a key measurement in helping you find your life purpose and fitting your life into the divine project.

Complexity Questions

The following questions might help your search to move from connections to complexity.

One by one, consider each of the significant connections you listed in the previous chapter, and then respond to all of the following questions:

- *How did the relationship add complexity to your life?*
- *How did you respond to it?*
- *Did you learn—or confirm—anything about yourself from it?*
- *Was it revelatory in some way of what you are becoming?*
- *Did it give you direction?*
- *Did it clarify something for you?*
- *Did it challenge you?*

In the previous chapter, Lou mentioned some of the qualities his friend and colleague Clare modeled for him. Clare also brought complexity into Lou's life. Here are his answers to some of the preceding questions.

> *How did this relationship add complexity to your life?*
> I was challenged to learn systems thinking and management philosophy, in neither of which had I any previous interest.
> *How did you respond to it?*
> I found the challenge exciting and very demanding.
> *Did you learn or confirm anything about yourself from it?*
> I discovered that, intuitively, I was already a systems thinker, though this was the first time I was learning the principles behind systems thinking. I was challenged to learn new terminology and to learn to present this new way of thinking using terms and examples ordinary

people could understand. I found I could do it and I enjoyed doing it.

Was it revelatory in some way of what you are becoming?

I also realized that Teilhard himself was intuitively a systems thinker, and with my new systems vocabulary I could explain Teilhard's ideas in ways no one had done before. For example, while Teilhard himself described the evolutionary law as "complexity-con-sciousness," it was clear that, from a systems thinking perspective, the law implied the preliminary elements of "attraction-connection" for much easier compre-hension. So I added them to the law.

Did it give you direction? Did it clarify something for you?

I realized that systems thinking would serve as a good foundation for thinking about spirituality and spiritual practice.

Did it challenge you?

It challenged me to begin rethinking all of my work and writing. I needed to come at everything with this new mindset and to do it consciously.

Digging Deeper into Complexity

When you are confronted with complexity in any form—complicated things, confusion, conflict, contradictions, dis-agreements, multiple opinions, several options, many different personalities, misunderstandings, and so on—which kinds of complexity do you feel ready to take on? And which would you rather avoid? Consider the following questions:

- *Which forms of complexity do not threaten you or feel overwhelming (though they may feel threatening or overwhelming to others)?*

87

- *Which forms of complexity do not take away your inner peace?*
- *Which forms of complexity do you feel confident in dealing with?*

For example, when Lou considers the tremendous complexity of today's automobile engines, he feels overwhelmed, while his nephew Alex, who works with vehicle engines as his occupation, loves the challenge of staring into a malfunctioning engine, especially one he has never seen before, finding out the source of the problem and how it can be fixed.

Again, when Lou sees two people bickering or heatedly disagreeing, he tends to turn the other way. He usually cannot make sense of the interpersonal problem, and he finds the anger energy emanating from the quarrelers frightening.[2] However, because Pat is an expert therapist in human interactive dynamics, she is quite attentive and ready for the encounter as she faces an arguing couple in her office. Like nephew Alex, Pat loves to find the roots of a problem and come up with alternative behaviors to help resolve it.

However, if Lou were asked to create a musical arrangement of a song for a forty-piece orchestra, he would relish the challenge, while wife Pat and nephew Alex would find it an impossible task.

Our daughter Serena is an actor whose favorite plays are attributed to Shakespeare. She has memorized various roles for a dozen of Shakespeare's long plays. She thinks little of the challenge such complex memorization requires, yet it is not something Alex, Pat, or Lou would even attempt.

The same gift of memory is true for symphonic soloists—pianists, violinists, flutists, and other musicians—who have memorized the solo parts of many entire symphonies and sonatas. A piano concerto, for instance, may contain tens of thousands of individual musical notes, each of which is to be played in proper order and in proper combinations at certain precise moments in the piece. And the soloists have all of those countless notes precisely arranged in their brains' memory.

Each of us has to deal with our own personal complexities. Think especially of the complexities facing parents who are trying to juggle careers and raise children, each with his or her own unique talents and complex personality, or new parents who come home from the hospital with a set of healthy active twins or triplets. No one is exempt from dealing with complexity.

The question is how to use complexity to help discern and identify our personal life purpose.

It will help if you reflect on the following three questions:

1. *What kinds of complexity are you most at ease with, most attracted to, most challenged by?*
2. *And in what areas of complexity are you willing—and even eager—to learn to deal with ever-increasing levels of complexity?*
3. *In which areas are you not afraid to try something new? To welcome the new and different? To welcome a challenge?*

You will get to read Lou's answers to these three important and revelatory questions later, but first here are some cautions.

Caution

Don't mistake anxiety before a task with distaste for it. For example, some people are meant to be public speakers but are at first afraid of standing at the podium. But once they overcome their fear—whatever its source—they go on to become excellent, captivating presenters.

If you feel called to a certain kind of work, don't be put off by such initial fears or stress. There is a big difference between "I have absolutely no wish to be a public speaker" and "I wish I could be a public speaker, but I'm afraid I can't do it really well."

When Pat first began making public presentations, she would break into a sweat, though she wanted very much and felt called to be a presenter. It didn't take very long before she found ways to calm herself before a talk and to find out what lay behind her fear of public speaking. She worked through the troubling issue and became a powerful presenter.

Another Possible Mistake

Don't simply assume that what you are good at automatically defines your purpose in life. Some people are good at many things, and this is where the art of discernment becomes crucial. Does each field in which you are gifted bring you joy or inner peace when you are practicing in that particular field? Perhaps some do and others don't.

For example, Lou is good in mathematics, and his Jesuit superiors at the time recognized it. They gave him the assignment to get a doctorate in math so that he could be a teacher in a Jesuit university. He was bright enough to win a scholarship and, in three years, a PhD in mathematical statistics. However, he had little deep interest in mathematics. Doing math was never a delight for him. Getting his degree was quite an achievement, because out of the sixty students who entered the graduate mathematics program when he did, only three of them received doctorates. Nevertheless, thinking about teaching math in a university never brought him inner peace. He felt a sense of accomplishment at completing the academic task, but no sense of delight or anticipation of pursuing mathematics as a lifelong career.

That was not where God was calling him to make his primary difference, even though his religious superiors believed so. Lou ultimately found his true purpose through theology and writing. But that purpose was not specifically theology and writing. What Lou finally discovered as his personal purpose was *helping people put their important but difficult ideas into words and formats that made those ideas accessible and of practical use to ordinary people.*

Some would call him a ghostwriter. But that is only part of his purpose in life. Besides helping people write books that they themselves could never write, he helps people structure their ideas, turning them into interesting lectures and workshops. He helps graduate students formulate their dissertations and shows them how to structure statistical models for their research.

Lou arrived at a formulation of his life purpose by (1) reflecting on the three complexity questions listed earlier and (2) identifying those areas of interest that fit with all three questions—and with the responses he gave to the attraction and connection questions as well as the connection questions. Here's how he put it together answering each of the three complexity questions.

Lou's Reflections

In reflecting on the first complexity question—*What kinds of complexity are you most at ease with, most attracted to, most challenged by?*—Lou answered "intellectual complexity" as the area he was most at ease with and to which he was most attracted. And when he asked himself *Why?*, he realized what he most enjoyed was organizing and systematizing intellectual complexity—in any field—and to present this organization in sentences and paragraphs (or diagrams) in ways that were intelligible and interesting to the ordinary reader or student. For example, as a ghostwriter, Lou has organized and systematized books for authors of books on psychology, relationships, communication, education, child rearing, theology, marketing, business, consciousness expansion, music, dreams, and even mathematics.

In a similar way, he also found challenging—and exciting—writing and orchestrating music for bands and orchestras.

In dealing with the second complexity question—*In what areas of complexity are you willing—and even eager—to learn to deal with ever increasing levels of complexity?*—Lou again selected intellectual complexity. In helping others write books on philosophy, theology, religion, history, and biography, for example, Lou has been challenged to do outside research, which expanded and increased his own knowledge. He often expressed his joy in his search for new knowledge by telling his wife and companions about his discoveries.

In music, Lou moved from orchestrating for instrumental combos and choirs to orchestrating for marching bands and concert orchestras. However, when faced with the complexities of learning new music-writing software, he balked. This new software program, unexplored, sits waiting on his computer.

In dealing with the third complexity question—*In which areas are you not afraid to try something new? To welcome the new and different? To welcome a challenge?*—Lou again listed "intellectual complexity" first and foremost. He has accepted the challenge of making understandable the many complex ideas of the Jesuit scientist-theologian-mystic, Pierre Teilhard de Chardin. He has jumped into a study of the Aramaic language, the language that Jesus spoke, in order to explore what other meanings this ancient language might reveal about Jesus's teachings.

In the end, the evolutionary challenge for each person is to introduce continually new complexity into his or her life, which forces us to become more welcoming, more integrative, more all-embracing, and more conscious. Your life purpose becomes clearer to you when you enjoy and even delight in the challenges complexity generates.

ALWAYS END YOUR REFLECTION IN GRATITUDE

Do not forget to acknowledge with gratitude the divine presence guiding you at each step of this process, for it is this loving spirit that most desires you to become aware of your unique purpose on Earth while helping fulfill the divine plan for creation. Your expressions of thanksgiving acknowledge that intimate connection between you and the divine presence guiding you.

NOTES

1. Reported by Ron Recinto in "The Lookout," *Yahoo News,* August 3, 2012.

2. Some might suggest that Lou would do well to face his issue of fear of strong emotion in others and develop his interpersonal skills in this area. Undoubtedly, therapeutic work in this area would help Lou develop a more well-rounded personality. However, the focus of this book is not on how to work through personality issues—a very laudable pursuit—but primarily on finding one's unique life purpose, a very different goal.

CHAPTER 14

CONSCIOUSNESS QUESTIONS

Before Each Session

Once again, you are beginning a new reflective session. Take a few moments to allow yourself to grow calm and, in any way you prefer, become aware of a divine loving presence guiding and supporting you in this endeavor.

In this divine presence, you may also wish to affirm your desire to work to help renew the face of the Earth, and your gratitude for the opportunity to make your unique contribution to the great evolutionary project.

Consciousness

You can find several definitions of consciousness, some of them very technical. However, here we are using a very simple one: *consciousness is awareness plus appropriate activity*. Both elements of the definition are important; the definition is applicable to all forms of life, from the most primitive bacteria to the most intelligent human being. As soon as a bacterium's outer surface becomes *aware* of a foreign object, it typically *acts appropriately* by moving away.

Especially for those of us who are human, consciousness is much more than simple awareness. Many people are aware of something, yet they do nothing to show or prove that they are aware. For example, some people are aware that certain foods are not healthy for them to eat, and if you asked them they could tell you so. They are clearly aware. Yet, the same people go right ahead and eat what they know is harmful to them, acting inappropriately. You can prove that your awareness has reached the stage of full consciousness only when you behave according to that awareness.

Nor is consciousness simply defined as appropriate action. Many people behave in a certain way that may be appropriate, yet they are unaware of why they are behaving in that way. For example, children often imitate the behavior and verbal expressions and prejudices of their parents, not knowing why they are doing so or what the behavior or words mean. They manifest appropriate behavior—or inappropriate behavior—but are not truly aware of what that behavior means or implies. For a person to possess consciousness, that person must both have an awareness *and* act appropriately on that awareness.

However, this chapter is about more than defining consciousness; it is focused on *raising or enlarging consciousness*, which means coming into *new* awareness and acting appropriately within that new awareness. The divine grand project, or plan, for Earth is challenging us to reach toward higher and higher levels of unity, requiring higher and higher levels of loving. In our religious tradition, God's name is Love. The divine Spirit is pure love and all-embracing love, so any project that the Spirit might undertake must be aimed at attaining as high a degree of inclusivity as possible. So, each higher level of consciousness will introduce you to a new level of loving, and at the same time integrate the lower levels.

Drivers of Consciousness Growth

What are some of the situations that typically evoke the emergence of a new level of consciousness and love, or at least an awareness of the need to reach a new level? Here are at least five, though there may be many more.

You have the chance to open up to a new level of consciousness

1. *When you cannot make sense of an important situation in your life;*
2. *When you cannot go forward unless you resolve an apparent conflict or contradiction;*
3. *When the situation requires that you give up something(s) that has been an ordinary and expected part of your life;*
4. *When you meet with an unexpected diminishment of yourself or someone dear to you, that is, when bad things happen;*
5. *When you spend time with a wise and loving person who is, in some particular way, more conscious than you.*[1]

These are five of the most common opportunities you have for growing in consciousness. The first four imply or involve some kind of struggle or conflict. The fifth works through simple receptivity, by listening, watching, and reflecting.

1. *Making Sense.* Things happen in everyone's life that don't make sense. Some examples might be: You do the right thing in a situation, and the result turns out wrong. You count on someone who has always been trustworthy, and they act unpredictably. You work hard and do your best at your job, and your supervisor gives you a poor evaluation. You belong to a church that professes love, compassion, and forgiveness as their primary values, yet when someone in good conscience interprets a church doctrine different from the official definition, the church officials excommunicate the person. You raise your children the best way you know how, and they turn out to do destructive or dan-

97

gerous things like bullying, joining gangs, breaking laws, becoming alcohol or drug addicted.

In each case, the problem cannot be understood or resolved at your current level of consciousness. At that current level, the problem makes no sense and offers no avenue of resolution. Only from the loving perspective of a new level of consciousness can such a problem be more fully perceived, reenvisioned, and lessons learned from it.

2. *Apparent Conflict or Contradiction.* Another kind of situation that calls for a growth in consciousness and love is when two people or two groups are in conflict, or there are two legitimate descriptions of a situation or problem, and the two appear to contradict each other. Two parents disagree on how to discipline a teen who has violated a curfew rule, yet the child must be disciplined. Two people at work disagree on how to balance a financial deficit, yet the deficit must be balanced. How do you grow into the mindset where you can hear both sides of the issue and see how they both fit? It requires a new level of consciousness. In cases like this, one is reminded of the Zen saying, "There is no solution; seek it lovingly."

3. *Losing Something Dear.* You want to excel in sports or science, and to do so you must give up much of the social life your friends enjoy. You want to provide the best for your new child, which means you will have to give up spending time or money on things for yourself. You want to accomplish or acquire something, but there always seems to be a big price to pay. Such situations challenge you to form a larger picture of your life and the lives of others around you, and to begin to look at things and make decisions from that larger perspective. Another way to evoke this new consciousness is to reflect on the question, *From a future*

perspective, in five or ten years will I look back on this situation and say, "I'm glad I made that decision"?

In the meantime, take a few moments to ask yourself questions like "Did I learn something important from that decision? How did that decision help shape or influence my life?"

4. *When Bad Things Happen.* So many things in life that happen to us are things we did not choose and would never want to happen. Sickness. Accidents. Losses. The death of a loved one. Bankruptcies. Foreclosures. Job loss. Demotions. Failures. Missed chances. Chapter 15 focuses on this painful opportunity to develop a higher level of consciousness and love.

5. *Being with a Wise and Loving Person.* Sometimes by listening to and observing such a person with openness and empathy, or just by spending time in his or her presence, we begin to resonate to the ways that person thinks and responds, and in that way we easily and naturally grow into new levels of consciousness without any struggle, almost by osmosis. During young childhood, we all learned to think and respond to situations the way our parents did. Those ways became ingrained and unconsciously part of our way of being. If we enjoyed wise and loving parents and learned wise and loving ways of thinking and behaving, we are lucky and should be grateful. For not everyone enjoyed such parents.

At any age, if you wish to grow in consciousness, expose yourself to good or inspiring people who think differently from you. Then, instead of saying, "I'm right and they're wrong," try saying, "We're both right, and my challenge is to embrace both perspectives, to see how both are true and contributing."

When this happens, you find yourself saying things like "I never knew that," "I never thought of that," "I never saw the situation from that perspective before," "I never knew ordinary people could accomplish such things."

But don't stop there. When a person or event proposes a powerful question to your mind or introduces you to a new idea, an idea you don't understand or know much about, that is the time to start thinking, reflecting, searching, researching, and asking more questions about that new idea. That is the divine Spirit in you inviting you to grow in consciousness, to integrate into your mind and heart whatever you discover.

Such consciousness-expanding new ideas can emerge on a retreat or when meditating on Scripture, but new ideas can also occur during a lecture, a workshop, a television documentary, a film, while reading a book, or even while having a conversation. Don't let those moments of awareness pass. Take time to digest what you are learning. Write in your journal what you have discovered.

As a counselor, Pat tries to develop consciousness in her clients. So, she usually asks clients, after a session ends, not to jump right into their cars and drive home, but to stay quiet for fifteen minutes in the waiting room to reflect and jot in a notebook what they want to remember from the session and think about further. If more questions arise during this reflection time, she suggests they write down those questions, think about them some more, maybe research them and bring the new learning to the next session. This is a sure way of holding on to the gift of insight and consciousness that is being given to you.

Summary

In each of these five kinds of situations, your challenge is to make a shift upward to a new way of thinking, feeling, and acting—a new level of consciousness—that is more loving and all-embracing. In this way, you grow into a more fully human person, as God would want you to be.

Only in this new consciousness can the important situation begin to make sense. Only in this way can the apparent conflict or contradiction be resolved. Only in this way can you willingly give up what needs to be let go of, and become able to see the wisdom and learning in the unexpected diminishment.

A Good Test

Here is a question that offers one way of identifying your divine call. When you think you have identified your unique purpose in life, ask yourself, *Does the state of consciousness that accompanies this purpose engender higher degrees of loving—an ever-widening, more all-embracing love? A love that includes nature and the environment? A love that includes people you don't like or disagree with? A love that includes the poor, the lonely, the forgotten, and the rejected in society? A love that is worldwide?*

As a human race, we are far from the stage of consciousness at which we are all purely loving one another—every other being. Yet, that total union in love is humanity's divinely inspired goal. As we attain each new stage of loving consciously, we move one step closer to that goal.

What you may first notice is that raising your consciousness to the next stage often requires a kind of symbolic death, the letting go of an older kind of thinking and behaving. The gymnast who would like to qualify for the Olympics will have to give up—die to— many years of ordinary fun and games that most students typically enjoy before and after school. The young musician who wishes to excel must practice daily, while his or her young friends enjoy spending time together. The research scientists conducting clinical trials, in order to keep a close watch on an experiment, must often forego free weekends or evenings out with friends.

In our society today, there are a number of stages of consciousness that are hard to give up. Most of them are ingrained in our cultural system.

Giving Up a Familiar Mindset

Specifically, most people today are at the stage of consciousness at which their primary value in life is winning. We characterize this competitive approach to life as a win/lose mindset. In this way of thinking, if someone wins, the others lose. This mindset prevails in sports, in school grades, in board games, in card games, in the workplace, in business, and even among nations. In fact, compete-to-win seems to be the everyday game of life. It encourages a domination-focused mindset—and society— where winner takes all.

Can we possibly even imagine a world where people have shifted their primary mindsets from a win/lose mentality to a win/win mentality? This shift happens to be the next stage of consciousness that the human race needs to reach. It is clear that the next stage of loving (win/win) needs to be a stage at which "everyone wins" or succeeds, at least in as many situations as possible.

Imagine how many cherished behaviors we in our culture would have to give up or let die within us in order to make this shift to a win/win mindset. We would have to give up our traditional grading system in schools. We would have to give up our obsession with ranking, comparing, and competing in sports: Who's the fastest, the biggest, the highest scorer? We would have to give up hierarchies in business. In politics, we would have to give up winning to dominate and shift to willingness to serve others, or at least to being appreciated individually for doing our best in any situation. As nations, we would have to give up war and domination.

We might describe this radical change as moving from a desire to have the first place or the top rank to choosing to use our talents and resources to help each other live to our personal and collective best physically, psychologically, and spiritually.

In place of what we gave up, we as a society would have to reach a radically new level of consciousness in order to be able to invent new kinds of sports, new card games, new board games, new systems of education, new relationships in the workplace, new ways of doing politics, as well as a new means of cooperation in business and among nations. We would promote peace academies over military ones. We would also focus on building health in all people, sharing food and other necessities, providing safe, healthy, growing, interactive communities.

This mindset shift requires an evolutionary process. It will happen by incremental improvements in the ways all of us live and think. And we need to do this continually and with consciousness—continual improvement in consciousness—however and whenever possible.

There are many other shifts in consciousness that need to happen before we develop a society where love is the predominant energy behind all that we do. For example, instead of thinking, "What's best for me?" I begin asking, "What's best for all concerned or for all those affected by my decision?"

It is difficult to formulate questions about a level of consciousness that is still currently out of reach. But, here is a question for your quiet reflection:

How is your personal life purpose geared to develop a continual growth in consciousness in you and in others?

Taking the Chance

In looking at these last two elements of the evolutionary law—complexity and consciousness—the temptation is to downplay them. One might think, "I'm cultivating attraction and connection, and that's enough. I don't really need to learn anything new." One might feel, "I do not need to give up the way I am used to thinking and the way I have been thinking all my life (win/lose) and go against everyone else's way of thinking." Facing the challenge of developing a new consciousness, people, even good-hearted people, find it tempting to stay with the status quo, to keep acting and thinking the way they have always thought and acted, convinced that "if it works, don't try to fix it."

The other side of the coin is to say, "I need to develop in complexity and consciousness, so I'll take the chance. I'll learn something new. I'll begin to shift my mindset. If it works well, I will try to make it work even better. I will try to continually improve the way I do things and live my life."

In the pursuit of higher consciousness, imagination is a most helpful human faculty. Teilhard tells us how to begin: "All we need is to imagine our ability to love developing until it embraces the totality of human beings and of the earth."

When you are inspired by some great purpose or some project that may appear extraordinary to you, your thoughts begin to break out of their traditional bonds. Your mind begins to transcend its former limitations, your consciousness begins to expand, and you find yourself in a new, great, and wonderful world. Forces, capacities, and talents in you that were unexplored or hidden and dormant before now become alive. You begin to have access to them, and you discover that you can accomplish things you never dreamed you could.

Expressing Gratitude

As always, end each reflective session with expressions of gratitude to the divine Spirit that continually guides and inspires you in this process. It is important to the grand divine project that you grow in awareness of the unique opportunities that are yours.

NOTE

1. We are indebted for this wonderfully rich fifth level of consciousness taught to us by the wise and gentle Linn family, Matt, Dennis, and Sheila, well-known authors of spirituality materials.

CHAPTER 15

WHEN BAD THINGS HAPPEN

Vocational Diminishments

What am I to do if some unplanned event happens to me that appears to affect my personal purpose in life?

A "bad thing" could be an unwelcome event or a diminishment, such as a personal illness, a terminal illness of one's child or spouse, the death of a partner or dear friend, a financial loss, a divorce, a serious conflict within a group leading to a breakup, getting fired from or losing a job, the closing of your company, failing a test or qualifying exam, or many other negative events.

Yet an unplanned event could also be an unexpected enhancement of your life or a shove in the direction of your life purpose—but not immediately recognized as such.

Consider the following life scenario: John was a celibate Catholic priest who fell deeply in love with a woman, and in order to marry her, he was forced to leave the priesthood, a role in life he cherished. Years later he realized he would never have discovered his true life purpose without that special love relationship. John developed a debilitating disease, which led him to a life of teaching others how to deal with—and sometimes overcome—aspects of their disabilities, allowing them to live more fulfilling lives.

Here is a simple process for dealing with an unplanned event.

WHY DID GOD MAKE ME?

STEP ONE

Whenever a major unplanned event occurs in your life, always treat it as a learning moment and an opportunity for spiritual and emotional growth. Ask yourself:

What can I learn or what have I learned from this experience?

- Recognize that such an unplanned event always adds *complexity* to your life.
- Recognize that, if you gain wisdom, insight, awareness, growth, or new experience from the event, you are growing in *consciousness*.
- Often, such an event establishes new *connections* for you—new people, new ideas, new associates, new perspectives, and so on.

Marjorie had just turned forty when her husband walked out of their marriage, leaving her with three children, all of elementary school age. The only thing her husband said upon leaving was that he didn't love her anymore and didn't want to deal with the children either. The abandonment seemed a total surprise to her, unexpected and unplanned for, leaving her very upset and confused. However, Marjorie managed to survive the difficult circumstances and raise her children with grace and wisdom.

We talked with her ten years later, when her oldest had graduated from college. When asked what she had learned from the divorce, she paused a moment before answering:

Well, I hadn't planned for his leaving me, and I was crushed and broken-hearted. I thought my life had ended. But, little by little, I discovered that I could cope on my own, even with complications and responsibilities I never had before. What at first seemed like a devastating loss—and it *was* in some ways—did set me free and challenged me to grow. I learned to manage my finances. I learned how to save money. I discovered who my true friends were. I rediscovered God.

I began helping out at my children's school, especially tutoring children, a role I grew to love that even led to further study and training. I was beginning to see more clearly what I would like to do with my life, how I could make a difference.

I also discovered that my children were very resilient and have become quite self-reliant and helpful to me. Tommy won a scholarship to college. Sarah learned to drive, and was able to help me do many chores and errands I couldn't have gotten done otherwise. Carole became quite a soccer player; she coached younger children, and in doing it felt valuable and productive. We probably grew closer to each other than we would have otherwise. We became a more cooperative and conscious family.

In her own way, Marjorie recognized how the loss of her husband brought complexity into her life, forced her to open up her awareness to new possibilities and perspectives, gave her some clarity in finding her life's direction, and introduced her to new connections with friends and colleagues as well as a conscious appreciation of family values.

In a similar way, many people who discover they have a terminal illness learn many new things about life. Perhaps for the first time, as our friend Suzanne did, they recognize the graces and blessings in ordinary things that they had felt entitled to and up until now had taken for granted before. In what were supposed to be the last four months of her illness, Suzanne developed a deeper gratitude for life itself and for the beauty surrounding her. She began to value the gift of each moment, the preciousness of friendship, the many opportunities—usually missed in the past—to show kindness, to treasure family, and to watch for the chance to make a difference in the world. As those months passed, she continued to live in an attitude of gratitude. Each day in her blog she would list things she was grateful for. Her list included mostly simple things like sunshine, a phone call, a flower, some food she managed to eat, a television show, a book she was reading, the family photo album, an afternoon nap. Her grateful attitude also affected her health. Although physicians had given her four months to live, she lived four more years. Amazed, the doctors wanted to know her secret. From her sickness, she had learned the life-giving power of being grateful rather than complaining.

She discovered that her purpose in life was, in part, to share her attitude of gratitude through her blog. Many who read her daily thanksgiving list, especially those with terminal illnesses, began to adopt her approach to life. She lived out her purpose of promoting her "Attitude of Gratitude" until her dying day.

STEP TWO

Ask yourself:

How does this unplanned event enrich, expand, or refocus my purpose, as I currently see it?

- How can what I learned, or the new connections I made, help enrich or expand my life purpose?
- How does it fit in with my life purpose as I currently see it? Does it challenge it, enrich it, or suggest I refocus it?
- How can I turn this "lemon" into "lemonade"?

Lou, who has been a trumpet player since he was nine years old, suffered a medical mishap during routine sinus surgery. The surgeon accidentally drilled a half-inch hole in the bone in his right eye wall. Because of this hole, Lou can no longer dare to put the strong inner pressure in his head that was essential in playing any wind instrument. One of Lou's life purposes is to perform music in bands to entertain people.

In asking himself this step 2 question, Lou was challenged to refocus his purpose. Because he could no longer perform as a trumpet player, how could he still perform music in the many community bands he played in? In a band, the only instruments that do not require head pressure when performing are the percussion instruments. So, Lou became a percussionist. In one band he played bass drum and crash cymbals; in another he played some accessory instruments, like tambourine, triangle, wood block, maracas, and so on; in a third band he learned to play the glockenspiel. Not only has this unplanned event—the hole in his eye wall—brought new experiences, new relationships, and new complexity to his life, but it has also brought a different consciousness, because the band's percussion section has a very different purpose in the ensemble from that of the trumpet section. In short, he had turned a "lemon" into "lemonade."

Lou's knowledge and appreciation of music helped him grow in consciousness and expanded his ways of loving.

CHAPTER 16

USING THE EVOLUTIONARY LAW AGAIN AND AGAIN

In the previous chapters, you have used the evolutionary Law of Attraction-Connection-Complexity-Consciousness to discern your primary life purpose—or some of the many roles and purposes that are part of your life. As we mentioned earlier, though it seems almost a contradiction, it is possible to have more than one primary life purpose, perhaps even a series of them.

For example, Lou has at least two, and they are quite different. One is simplifying complex intellectual ideas for people and another is performing music to make people happy. Pat had the purpose of being a good mother for many years. Once her children were educated, married, and raising their own families, she became a therapist. Now she describes her purpose as being an instrument of God's love and healing for those with traumas, emotional pain, or stress and spiritual issues. Our friend Clare has one primary life purpose in producing television documentaries that make people aware of problems in our society. At the same time, she has a purpose of being a connector of people. It is not unusual, when having a conversation with her for her to say, "You have to meet a friend of mine. You two have a lot in common. The next time you come for dinner, my friend will be there, so you can meet and exchange ideas."

Everyday Spirituality

We also stated that this same evolutionary law is operating in our everyday interactions. Each day, we strive to be *attractive* in body, mind, and spirit. Each day, we take advantage of making and building closer *connections* with each other and with new people. Each day, we are open to new *complexity* in our lives. Each day, we are open to having our *consciousness* expanded to new understandings, new ways of loving and enlarging the ways we learn and love. In other words, we are challenged to use the evolutionary Law of Attraction-Connection-Complexity-Consciousness each day of our lives. It becomes our guide in spirituality and daily decisions.

Making Major Decisions

We also want to remind you that you can use this same process in making major—and even some minor—decisions in your life. Shall you take this job or that one, if you happen to have a choice? Which one is more likely to further your personal life purpose or help you achieve what the divine Spirit within you hopes you will achieve?

Use the evolutionary law as a test. Which choice is more likely to increase *complexity* and *consciousness*? Can you detect a gentle, peaceful movement in your heart or spirit urging you more toward one choice than another?

Similarly, you may be dealing with decisions that will affect your life as well as the lives of many others. For example, should you marry this person or another? Should we bring another child into our family? What field of study should I major in during college or graduate school? Should I accept this appointment being offered to me? Should I enter into this regimen of chemotherapy or radiation? Should I move from this place to that to preserve my health or look for a better job? Should I enter religious life? Should I leave religious life? There are many other major decisions in life that may be helped by looking at the decision in light of the evolutionary Law of Attraction-Connection-Complexity-Consciousness.

A good example of this is the following story: Pat's daughter Eve had two job offers. One was a position with which she was very familiar and could do easily, the salary was quite attractive, and she already knew many of the people who would be her colleagues. She would have to do almost no preparation for the role, just jump in and go to work.

The other job required extensive training and, though it was related to her current work, would be new and challenging. She would have to take a number of courses to qualify for the job. She would undoubtedly need to be involved with many new people. The clients would be new and different. In short, she would have to deal with new connections and new complexity, requiring her to develop new levels of consciousness.

The discernment process was quite clear. To choose the second position would be to follow the evolutionary law, which is what she did.

Our son-in-law, whom we mentioned earlier, had been a very successful environmental lawyer in private practice *on the side of the environment*. He decided to take a great cut in salary to work for the governor's energy and environmental team. It was a big decision for him and his family, and an evolutionary move. Indeed, as one on the governor's team, he made many new *connections* not only among the team, but also with lawmakers and lobbyists. In being forced to deal with much greater *complexity*, he had his eyes as well as his mind opened up in many new ways, developing new levels of *consciousness*. For example, in drafting the wording of each environmental law for the state, he had to formulate legal and technical wording that would apply to many different localities and environmental needs throughout the state, as well as learn how to diplomatically present and describe each new law to lawmakers as well as to media people. He was frequently called upon to make statements to the media and appear before local town meetings to explain a law and answer questions from concerned citizens and businesspeople. He had to develop tact, openness, and charm to make himself more *attractive* to the people he had to deal with, especially those who were opposed to some new environmental regulations.

You are encouraged to use the evolutionary Law of Attraction-Connection-Complexity-Consciousness whenever making important decisions. It will serve as a helpful guide and keep you connected with your primary purpose in life. Usually, decisions that enrich your attraction, connections, complexity, and consciousness are most likely those in line with the divine project.

In making such decisions, you may also use Ignatius's traditional method of discernment, described in the following chapter.

CHAPTER 17

DISCERNMENT THROUGH INNER PEACE

Saint Ignatius Loyola in his original *Spiritual Exercises* offered a simple method of discerning God's will for you whenever you are facing a major life choice between two or more good and noble options.

Pat likes this classic discernment method; she has used it successfully with many of her counseling clients who had major decisions to make, and she wants to encourage the method's widespread use. It usually takes about a week to complete the process, but it can sometimes be done successfully in less time. This is how the process works.

Imagine you have two job offers, both of which are good and would be helpful in your life work. (You may substitute whatever kind of major life options you happen to be facing.) You want to choose the option that would best help promote the grand divine plan or project for creation (Pat often calls it "your soul's choice"), but you can't clearly tell which one the all-loving Spirit would want you to choose. This process is designed to give you a strong clue about which way to go.

By the way, this choice has nothing to do with sin; it assumes neither of the choices involves unethical behavior or encourages you to act in ways against your conscience. In this discernment process you are not making a choice between good and evil options, but between two good opportunities.

115

Step 1. Imagine you have chosen option 1 (put aside option 2 for the time being). Live for two days in your imagination as if you had formally made the choice for option 1. As you go about your day, watch your inner feelings. Be especially conscious of whether, with this choice, you feel some degree of inner peace, or you feel an inner disquiet. (Inner peace is a very subtle, gentle feeling that all is right with your life.) Make note of the quality and depth of your inner feelings during these two days. Note, too, the quality of your sleep and dream experiences.

Step 2. Give yourself at least one day of rest, that is, live one or two days as if you had not yet made any formal decision and are still undecided. This is to clear away any leftover feelings from step 1. This is a time for being open to making a choice, but not anxious about it.

Step 3. Imagine you have chosen option 2 (you have put option 1 aside). Live for two days in your imagination as if you had formally made the choice for option 2. As before, go about your daily activities, observing your inner feelings. Watch to see whether, living this way, you feel a sense of inner peace—or not.

Step 4. Consider which of the imagined options gave you the deepest inner peace. The option that gave you more inner peace, according to Ignatius, is likely the option the Spirit would like you to choose. Pat likes to describe this step as "listening to what your soul is telling you."

Ignatius is not guaranteeing that the result of this process definitely identifies the divine will for you, but is merely a strong clue or indication of the Holy Spirit at work in your soul.

Ultimately, no matter what discernment process you use, the choice remains yours. It is your free will that chooses. Always remember that divine Love will always work with whatever choice you make.

CHAPTER 18

CONCLUSION

Summarizing

If you have not yet done so, please take the time to summarize each of the four major sections of this discernment process. Gather together what you have learned, or confirmed, about your life purpose. Each of the four areas—*attraction, connection, complexity,* and *consciousness*—contributes to show how your life has been guided and directed by the Spirit of God. Those qualities and themes that recur frequently in your summary will help you formulate your life purpose. Spend some prayerfully reflective time on this process.

As best you can, try to formulate your life purpose in a single sentence. Go back to chapter 7 to review samples of such statements written by others. Use these as models for your own formulation. Notice, as you read these sample statements, that they do not specifically name a career path or occupation, such as surgeon, college professor, nurse, psychologist, minister, engineer, or lawyer, but rather they focus on the values or qualities that underlie the career choice, the deeper reasons for choosing this occupation. Those values and qualities are the key to your life purpose.

When you have formulated your statement, you may present it to the divine Presence in prayer. Notice if you feel at peace with it. If not, perhaps you can revise it in a slightly different way or give it a new focus.

When you find a statement of life purpose that feels right for you, you may rephrase it as a fundamental choice that you may make each morning to keep you aware of your life purpose. Some examples to consider:

I choose to live this day

- *as an instrument of God's healing in the world.*
- *working with young people, teaching them how to be good "team players."*
- *showing others who have the same disease as I have that they can still make a positive difference in the world.*
- *trying to put more love and compassion in the world.*
- *working for peace and justice.*

Thy Kingdom Come

Your life purpose will undoubtedly reflect your unique way of furthering what is trying to be accomplished in the world. It will fit in with the divine Law of Universal Love as well as with that law's evolutionary expression in Attraction-Connection-Complexity-Consciousness.

When Jesus prayed to the Creator God, "Thy Kingdom come!," he was using an Aramaic word for *kingdom* that had many levels of meaning.

For example, in Aramaic the word for *kingdom* may refer to the geographical area or boundaries of a nation, as in the place on Earth we call Italy or the land we call Argentina.

The word *kingdom* may also refer to the "realm," that is, all the different nations that are under the king's domain, as in the territories of the Roman Empire of Jesus's day or of the British Empire of the nineteenth century.

More likely, in the context of this prayer, Jesus was using a third meaning of *kingdom*, as "reign," which refers to the policies, values, and practices of a king or queen. In this sense, we might say, "During the reign of Queen Victoria, the British Empire was characterized by certain policies and practices, and accomplishments."

In this latter sense, God's reign is characterized by certain policies and practices. Jesus recognized that God's reign, in this sense, has not yet been fully accomplished, for in his prayer he does not say, "Thy Kingdom has already been fulfilled." Instead Jesus realized that the Creator's original vision for creation still has a way to go for its accomplishment. Jesus is calling for that fulfillment when he says, "Thy Kingdom come!"

Jesus reinforces the future-ness of God's reign in the next phrase of the prayer, when he says, "Thy will be done on Earth." That divine vision has not yet been carried out completely. There is still work to be done. The Spirit's vision for creation still waits for its fulfillment. More important for us, the grand project needs us to cooperate in its fulfillment. That is why each of us seeks to find our unique life purpose in this grand work. We are asked to live out the fullness of who we are.

The divine Spirit, which permeates and embraces all things in goodness and wisdom beyond comprehension, has given us the dignity and the co-responsibility of slowly turning the divine vision for creation into a living reality. There is no need to let the immensity of this project keep us from doing our little share, making our own contribution to the transformation of the world in love.

In this book we have used the evolutionary Law of Love as a way of searching for our unique purpose in life.

In the words of the Trappist monk, Basil Pennington, "There is no greater gift we can give people than to open out to them the way by which they can come to experience most intimately and constantly how much they are loved by God." And to show them how they can help fulfill the divine grand project for creation.

121

USING THE
EVOLUTIONARY
LAW OF ATTRACTION-
CONNECTION-
COMPLEXITY-
CONSCIOUSNESS

Attraction

FIRST ATTRACTION QUESTION

What are the people, places, events, activities, groups, and ideas that you find especially attractive?

This question covers six different dimensions of your human life: *people, places, events, activities, groups,* and *ideas.*

Each of these six dimensions generates a specific subquestion to reflect upon.

1. *What kinds of people do you prefer to spend time with?*
2. *What kinds of activities do you most enjoy?*
3. *What kinds of places do you tend to gravitate toward?*
4. *What kinds of events excite you? Or calm you? Or inspire you? Or seem most meaningful?*
5. *What kinds of groups would you choose to belong to? Or learn more about?*
6. *What kinds of ideas turn you on?*

FOUR REFLECTIVE STEPS FOR EACH QUESTION

Step 1. Try to list at least three or four answers to each
subquestion, but don't limit yourself. You may list ten
or more.

Step 2. What aspect or quality of each answer makes it
attractive to you?

Step 3. What is there within your special preferences for
this activity that most attracts you?

Step 4. In reviewing all your responses, look for similarities and themes.

SECOND ATTRACTION QUESTION

**What are some of the people, places, events, activities, groups,
and ideas that you find much less attractive?**

Again, there are six dimensions of this question, generating
six subquestions:

1. *What kinds of people do you prefer to stay away from?*
2. *What activities would you rather avoid?*
3. *What kinds of places do you prefer not to frequent?*
4. *What kinds of events sadden you? Or bore, frustrate,
   anger, or discourage you? Or have little meaning or significance to you?*
5. *What kinds of groups would you choose not to belong to?*
6. *What kinds of ideas anger or turn you off?*

Note: Carry out the Four Reflective Steps for each question.

THIRD ATTRACTION QUESTION

What is there about you that attracts people to you?

To help answer that basic question, look for positive
responses to the following:

1. What do people say about you?
2. What do they say directly to you?
3. What comments do people make to others about you? Compliments you received?

If you can't answer these questions from reflecting on your own experience, you might go directly to your friends and ask them:

- What is it about me that you like?
- Why do you like to spend time with me?
- What are the things you think I do best?

Connection

What are the personal connections that have helped shape your life so far?

In addition to persons, some important connections in your life may be with events, locations, personal experiences, information, books, or some other thing. In which case, substitute the "other thing" for "person" in each subquestion.

Once you have listed ten or more persons, groups, and other things, answer the following subquestions for each individual or item on your connection list:

- How would you describe this person's influence on you?
- What did you learn from this person?
- If it weren't for this individual,
  - What choices would you not have made?
  - What paths would you not have taken?
  - What other persons would you never have met or known?
  - What skills would you not have?
  - What information would you not know?

125

- *What areas of your life now would you be unacquainted with?*
- *What opportunities would you have missed?*

ALTERNATIVE

Take your notebook and at the top of the page write: *If it weren't for so-and-so...* [insert the person's or thing's name]. Then, complete that sentence with at least four or five different responses that apply to that person or thing. Do the same for each person on your list of persons or things that influenced your life.

Complexity

One by one, consider each of the significant connections you listed under connections, and respond to all of the following subquestions:

- *How did the relationship add complexity to your life?*
- *How did you respond to that added complexity?*
- *Did you learn—or confirm—anything about yourself from it?*
- *Was it revelatory in some way of what you are becoming?*
- *Did it give you direction?*
- *Did it clarify something for you?*
- *Did it challenge you? Help you grow?*

Here are a few more questions to reflect on regarding the force of complexity:

- *Which forms of complexity do not threaten you or feel overwhelming (though they may feel threatening or overwhelming to others)?*

- Which forms of complexity do not take away your inner peace?
- Which forms of complexity do you feel confident in dealing with?

After you list the forms of complexity in these three questions, it will help if you reflect on the following three subquestions:

1. What kinds of complexity are you most at ease with, most attracted to, most challenged by?
2. And in what areas of complexity are you willing—and even eager—to learn to deal with ever-increasing levels of complexity?
3. In which areas are you not afraid to try something new? To welcome the new and different? To welcome a challenge?

Consciousness

How is your personal life purpose geared to develop a continual growth in consciousness in you and in others?

WHEN BAD THINGS HAPPEN

Whenever a major unplanned event occurs in your life, always treat it as a learning moment provided by God. Ask yourself the following:

What can I learn or what have I learned from this experience?

- Recognize that such an unplanned event always adds *complexity* to your life.
- Recognize that, if you gain wisdom, insight, awareness, growth, or new experience from the event, you are growing in *consciousness*.

- Often such an event establishes new *connections* for you—new people, new ideas, new associates, new perspectives, and so on.

How does this unplanned event enrich, expand, or refocus my purpose, as I currently see it?

- How can what I learned, or the new connections I made, help enrich or expand my life purpose?
- How does it fit in with my life purpose as I currently see it? Does it challenge it, enrich it, or suggest I refocus my purpose?
- How can I turn this "lemon" into "lemonade"?

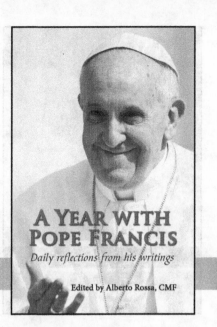

A YEAR WITH POPE FRANCIS
Daily Reflections from His Writings
Edited by Alberto Rossa, CMF

This pocket-sized volume contains a treasure of
reflections and quotations from beloved Pope Francis
for each day of the year. These words from the pope
will strengthen you in faith, build you up in hope,
and bring you closer to God.

978-0-8091-4889-9   Paperback

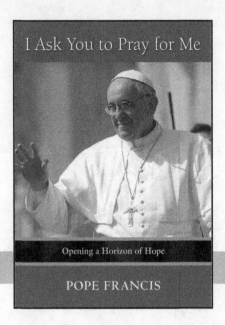

I ASK YOU TO PRAY FOR ME
Opening a Horizon of Hope
Pope Francis

Taken from his first official statements,
this book offers a glimpse into the mind and heart
of our new pope, in his own words.

978-0-8091-4859-2   Paperback

"With wonderfully simple advice like, 'if it helps, do it; if it doesn't, don't' and plenty of at times laugh-out-loud anecdotes, Leonard offers a fresh and engaging perspective on the richness and diversity of one of the church's greatest traditions. For all who struggle to maintain their own personal relationship with God, *Why Bother Praying?* is an answer to their prayers—especially if they are reluctant to say them."

—Scott Alessi, Managing Editor,
U.S. Catholic

WHY BOTHER PRAYING?
Richard Leonard, SJ

Here is a book for everyone who wonders how to pray, everyone who wonders what happens when you pray, and everyone who wonders if God hears our prayers.

"This brilliant work by a gifted priest is one of the best books you will ever read on the question of suffering—in other words, one of the best books you will ever read on the spiritual life. Richard Leonard, a Jesuit priest and author whose family has known intense suffering, gently invites readers to confront the important questions that every believer will face one day. Wise, insightful, pastoral, original, experienced, and never settling for easy answers, Father Leonard is the compassionate guide that all of us wish we had in times of pain. This profound book is for anyone who will face suffering in life—that is, everyone."

—James Martin, SJ, author of *Becoming Who You Are*

978-0-8091-4803-5   Paperback

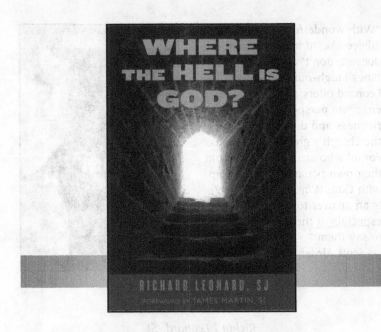

WHERE THE HELL IS GOD?

Richard Leonard, SJ; foreword by James Martin, SJ

Combines professional insights along with the author's
own experience and insights to speculate on how believers
can make sense of their Christian faith when confronted
with tragedy and suffering.

978-1-58768-060-1   Paperback
978-0-8091-4749-6   Large Print Edition

DANCING STANDING STILL
Healing the World from a Place of Prayer;
A New Edition of *A Lever and a Place to Stand*
Richard Rohr
with a foreword by James Martin, SJ

Now in a new edition, this bestseller explores the challenges, the rewards, the call, and the possibilities of integrating a sincere inner life with an active life of engagement with the pain of the world.

978-0-8091-4867-7   Paperback

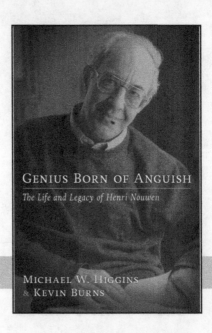

GENIUS BORN OF ANGUISH
The Life and Legacy of Henri Nouwen
Michael W. Higgins and Kevin Burns

An intimate look at this important spiritual writer's life,
enriched with the personal accounts of some of the people
closest to him: friends, family, and colleagues.
A twelve-page photo section is included.

978-0-8091-4785-4   Paperback

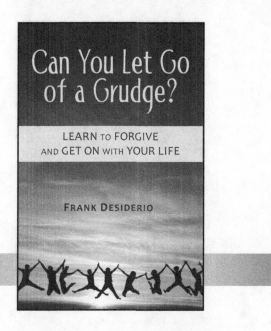

CAN YOU LET GO OF A GRUDGE?
Learn to Forgive and Get on with Your Life
Frank Desiderio, CSP Paperback

In this guide through the issues that prevent us from
forgiving, Frank Desiderio presents a five-step process
that will help the reader to let go of a grudge and,
if it's the right thing to do, be reconciled.

978-0-8091-4844-8 Paperback

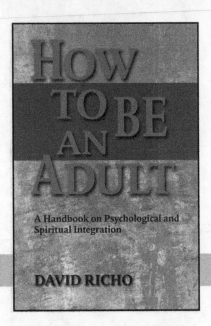

HOW TO BE AN ADULT
A Handbook on Psychological and Spiritual Integration
David Richo

Using the metaphor of the heroic journey—
departure, struggle, and return—the author shows
readers the way to psychological and spiritual health.

0-8091-3223-0   Paperback

BECOMING WHO YOU ARE
Insights on the True Self from
Thomas Merton and Other Saints
James Martin, SJ

By meditating on personal examples from the author's life, as well as reflecting on the inspirational life and writings of Thomas Merton, stories from the Gospels, as well as the lives of other holy men and women (among them, Henri Nouwen, Therese of Lisieux, and Pope John XXIII) the reader will see how becoming who you are, and becoming the person that God created, is a simple path to happiness, peace of mind, and even sanctity.

1-58768-036-X Paperback

THE GRATITUDE FACTOR
Enhancing Your Life through Grateful Living
Charles M. Shelton, PhD

Explores the significance of gratitude for one's
personal and spiritual life, offering a unique blend
of the latest research and practical strategies and
exercises to foster a grateful heart.

978-1-58768-063-2   Paperback

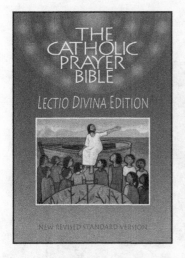
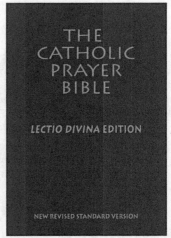

THE CATHOLIC PRAYER BIBLE (NRSV)
Lectio Divina Edition
Paulist Press

An ideal Bible for anyone who desires to reflect on
the individual stories and chapters of just one, or even all,
of the biblical books, while being led to prayer
through meditation on that biblical passage.

978-0-8091-0587-8   Hardcover

978-0-8091-4663-5   Paperback

978-0-8091-4766-3   Deluxe Edition
(Gilded pages; bonded leather cover—navy)

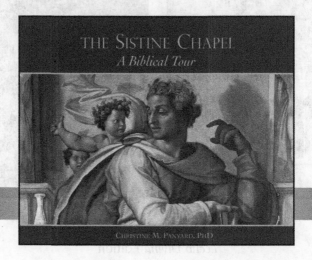

THE SISTINE CHAPEL
A Biblical Tour
Christine M. Panyard, PhD

An extraordinarily beautiful and unique book that
brings together the paintings from the ceiling and wall
over the altar of the Sistine Chapel with their
foundation in Holy Scripture.

978-0-8091-0593-9 Hardcover